FIRST DAYS OF GRANDPARENTING

DEVOTIONS TO SHARE YOUR PRIDE AND JOY

MARY HARWELL SAYLER

Nashville, Tennessee

Printed in the United States of America

4253-84
0-8054-5384-9

Dewey Decimal Classification: 242.65
Subject Heading: Devotional Literature \ Grandparent and Child
Library of Congress Card Catalog Number: 94-42381

Library of Congress Cataloging-in-Publication Data

Sayler, Mary Harwell.
First days of grandparenting : devotions to share your pride and joy / Mary Harwell Sayler.
p. cm.
ISBN 0-8054-5384-9
1. Grandparents—Prayer-books and devotions—English. 2. Devotional calendars. 3. Spiritual life—Christianity. I. Title.
BV4845.S279 1995
242'.645—dc20 94-42381
CIP

To Bibba, Elizabeth Trice,

who let us

be her children, too,

as we grew up in Lewisburg, Tennessee.

And to others around the country

who helped to parent my family spiritually:

Charlotte Fitzgerald, Church of Christ

The Rev. Homer Peden, United Methodist Church

Dr. Warren Porter, United Presbyterian Church

Rev. John Farrar, Southern Baptist Church

Rev. Horace Doudy, Presbyterian Church

Rev. David Suellau, Episcopal Church

Sue Wiatt, There Is More Ministries

Rev. Andrew Krumbhaar, Episcopal Church

Rev. Francis MacNutt, Roman Catholic Church

Rev. Terry Fulham, Episcopal Church

Minnie Coleman, There Is More Ministries

Rev. Keith Elliott and the members of

Pershing Avenue Christian, Orlando, Florida

—God bless each of you for the love and wisdom you've bequeathed to me and my family, now and in the generations still to come in Jesus' name.

Introduction

Does it seem like yesterday or a thousand years ago that your child first came to be? Timeless, your love now reaches beyond decades of parenting into an everlasting realm. You're a grandparent. New life goes on! As it goes, you may be inclined to want to change a thing or two! Most people do. Yet, like Mary, as she sat at Jesus' feet, you have the better part, kept and retained. You have the Lord's embrace in these first days of grandparenting and in the blessed years to come.

As you begin this new phase of your life—grandparenting—you may feel totally unprepared! Or you may have been waiting years for the opportunity. Either way, this is not only a new phase of life to enjoy, but a time to learn new things about yourself, your family, and your relationship with God.

No matter how well you know God's Word, you always have more to learn! So, before you begin this journey of devotion to God and your family, find a translation of the Bible that you'd love to take along. If you have a cover-worn favorite, great! But, to see aspects of God's Word you might not have noticed before, find a version that speaks to you with fresh and even startling impact. You have many fine translations from which to choose. In the following pages, you'll find Scripture from these versions of the Bible:

KJV—*King James Version*

NCV—*New Century Version*

NRSV—*New Revised Standard Version*

TEV—*Today's English Version* (also known as the *Good News Bible*).

Day 1

And suddenly there was with the angel a multitude of the heavenly host, praising God, and saying, "Glory to God in the highest heaven, and on earth peace among those whom he favors!"

Luke 2:13–14, NRSV

You're not dreaming. It's really happening. Sometime in the last few months, your son or daughter has given you the news, "Guess what, Mom/Dad? We're going to have a baby!"

And suddenly you seemed to hear a multitude of heavenly host, praising God and saying, "Glory to God in the highest heaven." That's assuming, of course, you'd been waiting to hear this news for a while!

If not, you may be having some unsettling feelings. You might be concerned if the baby will be born to a single parent or into a home struggling with marital, financial, or health problems. You might even feel as though the baby's arrival won't be announced by heavenly voices but by tabloids in a grocery store checkout line!

Whether you're annoyed or overjoyed, the big news is this: *You're* about to have a baby, a perfectly *grand* baby! And that's a grand and glorious reason for praising God.

Thank God for His life, His inheritance at work in you and your family. Thank Him for favoring you with His peace—a peace that not only passes understanding but can be passed on, from one family member to another and one generation to the next. Thank God for the coming of your first grandchild.

Prayer: Dear heavenly Father, help me to be like an angel in welcoming this child! Help me to draw a multitude of family members together in the love, joy, and peace of Jesus' name.

Journey with God: Before your grandchild arrives, begin these first days of grandparenting in the daily presence, power, and peace of the Lord. To help, this book includes Scripture verses for you to dwell on and consider. In the spaces provided each day, jot down thoughts as they come to you. Begin journaling by taking note of whether and/or why you're praising and giving thanks to God.

In the beginning God created the heaven and the earth.

Genesis 1:1, KJV

"I don't think I'm ready for this! Sure, I'm excited about the baby, but I'm not *old* enough to be a grandparent!"

Of course, you're not! No one is. Yet one year leaps to the next, and another generation begins without waiting for you to get prepared. But, thank God, He did not leave you without help or hope! In His intricate and infinitely wise plan, God created time. He brought to life the days and hours without treating them as something to be grabbed from a fast-food lane. He gave life time to seed, root, and unfurl. So unless your out-of-town or out-of-touch son or daughter has waited to spring the big news from a delivery room, God has given you several months to get used to the idea of being a grandparent!

In the beginning, God created heaven and earth and all that is within them. He created male and female. He created the promise of good things to come. He created your family, and, ever since, He's been right there to help.

Although you might not be sure you're ready to be a grandparent, God knows you are. Why? *He's ready* for you! He brought you to this time and place—not to bring up young children but to *upbring* and *uplift* your family to Him.

So, as you approach these first days of grandparenting, first approach the Lord. Let Him speak to you of past memories—perhaps in need of healing. Let Him bring to light your present attitudes and current expectations of yourself and your children. Let Him create His future for your family—starting right here on earth in His heavenly time and place!

Prayer: Dear Father, help me to be ready for Your words to me and Your new life to us in Jesus' name.

Journey with God: The thought of being a grandparent brings excitement and, sometimes, dismay. In the space below, tell God how you feel today about grandparenting. Thank Him for His perfect timing for your family. If you're unsure of that, ask Him to help you see the evidence of it.

____

____

____

____

____

____

____

____

They said to her,
"None of your relatives has
this name."
Then they began motioning to his
father to find out what name he
wanted to give him.

Luke 1:61–62, NRSV

Has your son or daughter decided what to call the baby? Has he or she discussed potential names with you?

Most new parents want to pick out a name by themselves, and, of course, they have every right to do so. You probably had that privilege when your child arrived. Now, your son or daughter gets a turn.

Hopefully, the choice will be one you really like, but it might sound like the worst name you have ever heard! If so, be careful not to hurt your son or daughter's feelings. However, that doesn't mean your lips are sealed as tightly as Zechariah's were before John the Baptist's birth!

Lightly broach the subject of names by asking your child and his or her spouse if they would like a list of your ancestors. If so, include your own or your mother's maiden name. Use this opportunity to introduce relatives from both sides of your family, especially people your child can't meet or recall but ones who meant a lot to you. As you note dates and places of births, occupations, and deaths, add some anecdotes, personal memories, or family photographs to make each person more "alive" to your child.

While you're on the subject of names, toss in your favorites too. Then, once you've offered your list of ancestors and name suggestions, seal the subject and your lips with prayer!

Eventually, your son or daughter might ask, "How do you like the name we picked?" And you won't lie! You will have *pre-prayed* to accept their final choice, even if you have to say, "What an unusual name! Tell me about it."

Prayer: Dear God, please help me to let my child have the privilege, fun, and power involved in the choosing of names! Help me to accept the choice in the blessed name of Jesus.

Journey with God: Have some of your child's choices been difficult to accept? Ask God to make clear to you what you're to keep quiet about and what you're to say.

The true children of God are those who let God's Spirit lead them. The Spirit that we received is not a spirit that makes us slaves again to fear. The Spirit that we have makes us children of God. And with that Spirit we say, "Father, dear Father."

Romans 8:14–15, NCV

One of the privileges of being a grandparent is naming yourself! You decide what you want to be called, and then you let your children know.

"Grandmother," "Grandfather" have a loving, respectful tone. "Gran," "Granny," "Gramma," "Grandpa," "Gramps" sound affectionately old-fashioned. "Mammy," "Pappy" sound lively. "Mother ___," "Mama ___," "Daddy ___," "Papa ___" (fill in the blank with your first, last, or nickname) sound youthful.

Most likely, you'll wait two or three years before your grandchild calls you anything, but your child may want to get in the habit right away! So, as you think about what you prefer to be called, find a name that sounds like you—and like the *relationship* you want to have with your grandchild. From your very first days of grandparenting, you decide how you want to be known.

God wants to be known as "Father." Jesus' prayers and other translations of the above Scripture use the Aramaic word *Abba*, best translated as "Daddy" or perhaps "Poppa." This name shows the intimate, affectionate, life-giving, healthy relationship your heavenly Father wants to have with His children.

In the name of Jesus and the power of His Holy Spirit, God brings into His spiritual family all who come to Him. He promises an inheritance of eternal life as He adopts you into His kingdom, starting now! Your Holy Father, your heavenly "Daddy," wants you to be His child. With "Poppa," you have nothing to fear.

Prayer: Oh, Poppa! I want to climb into Your arms and have every fear just flee! Help me to be led by Your Spirit into a close, family relationship with You in Jesus' name.

Journey with God: As you think about the name you want to be called someday, consider the type of relationship you'd like to have with your grandchild. Then remember the kind of relationship God wants you to have. Ask Him to bring to your mind the affectionate name He wants you to call Him.

____

____

____

____

____

____

____

____

Those who go to God Most High
for safety will be protected
by God All-Powerful.

Psalm 91:1, NCV

This is it! It's time! Are you ready for a labor of love? Are you prepared to spend long, hard hours praying for your family?

If you want to be with your daughter or daughter-in-law as she goes into labor, be sure to get permission from her and the hospital. You'll also need to be honest about your ability to stay calm in the delivery room.

When exciting things happen, people just naturally get excited! Some hold their emotions in check enough to have a calming effect on the soon-to-be-parents. Others have helpful medical training or physical stamina. But those who faint at the sight of blood or weep at the sound of someone else's pain also have a job to do—in the waiting room!

Careers often take young people far from home, so maybe you can't get within five hundred miles of the hospital. But you can always get to God! Whatever state you or your family find yourselves in—a state of emotionalism or a state like Louisiana—you can go to the Lord in prayer. You don't have to wait until you're laboring for your family's physical, mental, or spiritual health. Keep them in constant prayer as God brings them to your mind throughout each day.

Pray for your child and spouse to want the wisdom and love needed to practice good parenting skills—ones based on godly, Bible principles. Pray for their family's health, well-being, and protection of their bodies, minds, and spirits. Pray for your grandbaby's safe arrival—into this world and into the hearts of all who will encounter this new and blessed life.

Prayer: All-Powerful God, I want to protect my family from harm, but there's so little I can do! They need You, Lord! I trust Your willingness, ability, and presence to bless each member of my family—born and unborn. Please guide the doctor and medical staff, and help me to know what You want me to do. Thank You for Your labor of love and the safe delivery of my family into Your kingdom in Jesus' name.

Journey with God: Write a prayer for your family's well-being.

____

____

____

____

____

____

____

Day 6

I will praise thee, for I am fearfully and wonderfully made: marvelous are thy works; and that my soul knoweth right well.

Psalm 139:14, KJV

Congratulations! With God's help (and, of course, your child's) you've produced a wonderful, marvelous grandbaby! Let this good news sink deeply into your spirit and uplift your soul—your emotions, attitudes, and choices. Let this announcement of your grandchild's birth herald your thanksgiving, joy, and praise.

Hopefully, you're happy about this new boy or girl—simply delighted! But, if you sense even a twinge of disappointment, don't try to hide your feelings from yourself or God! Immediately, release them to Him alone. Then you will be ready to see and celebrate the wondrous sight before you.

Oh, look! See those little toes and baby fingers! How precious! See those feathery eyelashes and incredibly big, round eyes! Aren't they marvelous and unique? Aren't they exactly what your heavenly Father had in mind?

It's awesome! Your grandchild is fearfully, wonderfully made. Even if you can't be there to see for yourself, you can take God's Word for it! He's known all along what your new grandson or granddaughter would look like. From the moment of conception, He has cradled this child in the womb. Now, He's safely brought this new life into your life!

Thank God. Praise Him. Give Him your misgivings, and be done with any doubts or disappointments. From your very first moments of grandparenting, let nothing hinder your soul and spirit from uplifting and upbringing this child to God.

Prayer: Heavenly Father, You do such good work! Forgive me for doubting You or wanting You to do things my way. Thank You for Your wondrous gift of life in Jesus' name.

Journey with God: Talk with God about any flaws you see or fears you have for your grandchild. Thank Him for His perfect will for your family and the perfection found only in His Son, Jesus Christ.

Day 7

My darling, everything about you is beautiful. There is nothing at all wrong with you.

Song of Solomon 4:7, NCV

Labor got its name for a very good reason: It's hard work! Despite being laborious and fatiguing, it's also highly productive. Therefore, your daughter or daughter-in-law deserves to be acknowledged for doing such good work!

If you can't be with her in person, be there immediately with your thoughtfulness by ordering her favorite flowers. Or send a bouquet of colorful balloons with a note saying, "Thanks!" Telephone calls and cards of appreciation also help you to express your gratitude to her for giving you such a lovely gift—your very first grandchild!

Since childbirth can be rather strenuous, your daughter or daughter-in-law will not be at her physical best. Her hair will be a mess. She'll probably have on less powder than the baby does, and she might look absolutely exhausted—mainly because she is! So, before you visit, remind yourself to find *something* encouraging to say.

If your "daughter-in-love" had a difficult labor, she will be stunned by her appearance. Even if the delivery went speedily and well, she'll still be disappointed to see that her tummy isn't flat! Lord willing, her body will soon return to normal. Meanwhile, plenty of reassurance, along with your thanks, will let her know there's nothing wrong with how she looks. Everything about her appearance is just as it should be. Everything is all right. This is the mother of your very first grandchild! Who or what could be more beautiful?

Prayer: Dear God, thank You so much for my grandbaby's lovely mother! Please give me healing, helpful words to uplift her into Your love. Help her to recover speedily in Jesus' name.

Journey with God: Talk with God about the mother of your grandchild. Ask Him to give you His words to say and pray.

Record your prayer here.

"I am the LORD who created you;
from the time you were born,
I have helped you. Do not be afraid;
you are my servant,
my chosen people
whom I love."

Isaiah 44:2, TEV

How is your son or son-in-law holding up? Even if the doctor vowed, "Everything's normal," the new dad might not be convinced! At the moment, he's too new to fatherhood to recognize "normal" in anything!

Despite his cheery voice or face, he may be feeling a little afraid. He might be worried about his family's health or his own ability to be a good father and a supportive spouse. Talking about how he feels can help—assuming this isn't new for him, too!

If he's not used to communicating his fears or feelings, he might appreciate hearing how scared you were or how you fretted when your first child arrived. The idea is not for you to add to his worries, but to let him know what "normal" is—which generally means, "There's nothing to worry about!"

As you embrace him physically—or—brace him with your loving words by phone—use the time to remind him of God's presence. If he expresses worry, help him to see that God doesn't abandon the life He brings! No matter how "abnormal" a moment seems, God can be trusted to bring good.

our "son-in-love," this is not the time for ns! But offer to pray with him about any s, and also pray for him alone by yourself. w how glad you are that he's part of your life; point of telling him, "I appreciate you. I'm proud of yo hanks for giving me such a beautiful grandchild."

Prayer: Heavenly Father, thank You for loving us, Your chosen people. Help me to express Your love to the family You have chosen for me in Jesus' name.

Journey with God: As you journal, list every concern you have for the mental, physical, and spiritual health of your son or son-in-law. Then take time to pray about these specific concerns you've listed.

Day 9

LORD, help me control my tongue.
Help me be careful about what I say.

Psalm 141:3, NCV

So, who do you think the baby looks like? Your son or daughter, of course, and, well, maybe just a little like you. . . .

Whether your new grandbaby has come to your family by birth or adoption, you want him or her to resemble you in some way. It's not that you think you're the best-looking person in the whole world! But, like most people, you just want to see some connection between yourself and your offspring. You want an immediate, familiar bond with this tiny, new person you've just begun to know and love.

Naturally, your child's in-laws feel the same! They also want a sense of attachment or a means of identifying the baby with themselves. After all, this little one is their grandchild too!

With so many relatives to cover, take care not to tug too much of the baby's looks onto your side of the family! If in-laws make that difficult, pray for God's help to be gracious in everything you say and do regarding the people in this new baby's life.

Pray, too, that God will enable you to see appealing traits that remind you of each close member on both sides of the family—especially those who seem to toss out hints!

For instance, if someone says, "Don't you think the baby has my eyes?" they're obviously going for a "Yes!" So, don't lie! Squint! Ask God to give you His love to see the similarities between your grandchild and his or her other grandparents. Ask Him to help you accept the people who aren't even related to you and just do not resemble you at all!

Prayer: Dear Father, help me to make peace and bring love to my family and in-laws in Jesus' name.

Journey with God: Before praying for your child's in-laws, ask God to bring to your mind the prayers He most wants you to pray. Write your thoughts here.

*Honor your father and your mother,
so that your days may be long
in the land that the LORD your God
is giving you.*

Exodus 20:12, NRSV

Have you held the baby yet? When you embrace your very first grandchild for the very first time, you might be overcome with emotion. No wonder! This is such a joyous, exciting occasion that you'll remember these feelings years from now, even if other details don't seem too clear!

In a twinkling, you step into the past—remembering the first time you held your own newborn child. Yet in this timeless moment, you might also glimpse some things to come—envisioning generations of love, ascending and descending before you as on a ladder—until gravity suddenly sets you on the bottom rung!

"Mom/Dad, did you remember to wash your hands first?"

"Don't kiss the face, OK? Kiss the forehead."

"Oh! Be careful of the baby's neck. It's wobbly."

"Watch out for the soft spot!"

Nervously, new parents will rattle off a list of basic instructions as though you'd never done this in your life! If you didn't know your child so well or weren't so experienced with babies, you might be offended! Instead, you see this as a joyous occasion for thanking God!

Thank Him for giving you a child who wants to do what's best for a newborn. Thank Him for the love and care shown in your family. Thank Him for this new generation. Thank Him for helping you get off to such a good start!

In these first days of grandparenting, your initial task has now begun. Of course, you'll wash your hands. You'll kiss the forehead. You'll obey your child's instructions. For as you *honor* these requests, you set a standard that your grandchild can someday follow in honoring this new father and mother. On behalf of this baby, that's the pattern you've begun.

Prayer: Father, help me to honor You and my child's parental rights in Jesus' name!

Journey with God: Ask God for His instructions on ways you're to set an honorable example for your new grandchild. Then record them in the form of a letter to your grandchild.

____

____

____

____

____

____

____

____

Day 11

So God created humankind in his image, in the image of God he created them; male and female he created them.

Genesis 1:27, NRSV

Were you afraid you'd forgotten everything you used to know about babies? Aren't you relieved to see how quickly you remembered? That's great! Take lots of credit, and give every bit of it to God!

Not only has your Heavenly Father created a beautiful grandchild in His image, He also created you. God gave you time, talent, and an ongoing ability to learn, remember, and appropriately use what you've been taught.

But, maybe you don't feel as though you've learned much. Maybe you detect no resemblance between yourself and God. Or, maybe you think your child considers you the world's worst parent! If you hold onto such thoughts, you might be right!

God said He created you in His image; therefore, He did! That's His word on the subject—one you can steadily hold before you, no matter what! So, use it to replace any poor likeness of God you've kept as a mental picture of yourself.

Because you're human, you've distorted God's reflection of Himself in you. Everyone has! No one is exempt from this reality but Christ. He alone has remained God's true and perfect likeness. Therefore, in Him, you can give up that poor reflection of yourself and your parenting days!

Let go of marred memories. If you've wronged your child and never confessed it to God, do so now. Even if something horrendous happened years ago, the smudge will remain until you ask Jesus Christ to wipe it clean. He will! Then, as you see His love and forgiveness in your mirror, you will recognize God's image, restored and reflected in you.

Prayer: Oh Lord, I wish I'd handled some things differently as a parent! Forgive me. Help my child to forgive me too, and please help me to forgive myself. In Jesus' name, I choose to let go of any poor image of myself in exchange for Your image of me, made whole by the love of Christ.

Journey with God: Talk with God about anything you wish you'd done differently as a parent. Listen to His forgiving word.

____

____

____

____

____

____

____

____

Day 12

Then God said, "Let us make humankind in our image, according to our likeness."

Genesis 1:26, NRSV

God created His children in His image, so parents often try to copy the idea! At times, you've wished your son or daughter would be a little more like you, haven't you? Well, now that he or she is a parent, you might wish so a lot more!

Sometimes, differing personalities affect parents and children as each tries very hard to see the other's point of view. But most parents usually want their children to follow their example and behave!

If your child hasn't presented a perfect picture of your family, you might have some additional concerns now that the baby has arrived. Lifestyles involving flagrant disobedience to God's Word certainly are cause for concern and prayer. As a loving parent, you naturally want what's best for your family. So, you want your son or daughter to reflect at least some resemblance of God in their choices and their lives.

The more your child and his or her spouse have turned from what you'd hoped, wanted, or expected, the less comfortable you'll be in your relationship with them. But even if you have solid, biblical reasons for disliking their choices, you can prayerfully disapprove the *lifestyle*—not the *life.*

Ask God to bring into your view, His image and likeness of your family. According to His image, He imagines things about your family that you might not know or see. According to His likeness, He likes each of you! So don't be concerned if your son or daughter isn't at all like you—or isn't like you had once imagined he or she would be! Look to see—*pray* to see—your child take after the Father who is in heaven!

Prayer: Heavenly Father, I want to take after You! I want to be like You. Help me to reflect Your love, acceptance, and forgiveness of my family in the power of Jesus' name.

Journey with God: Do you have an out-of-focus picture of your family? Ask God to help you see each individual family member separate from the choices they make. Pray about any distorted features you see—not ones unlike you, but the ones unlike God.

____

____

____

____

____

____

____

Day 13

What we see now is like a dim image in a mirror; then we shall see face-to-face. What I know now is only partial; then it will be complete—as complete as God's knowledge of me.

1 Corinthians 13:12, TEV

Guess what you've done! You've cleaned out a closetful of regrets to make room for new life born into your family.

By seeking forgiveness, you began to look at yourself as God does. By seeing yourself in Christ, you stood before His holiness—like a mirror that shows where you went wrong. In His own flawless image, Jesus Christ perfected you. Now, when God looks at you, He sees the reflection of His Son!

Maybe your son or daughter and spouse won't see that just yet! Maybe they'll only see your mistakes and be worried they'll repeat them! Perhaps they will. Nevertheless, you can pray for a timely opportunity to seek their forgiveness.

Receiving your child's forgiveness might not change much for you. You've already straightened things out with God, so past sins or mistakes no longer hold power over you! However, your family may still need to forgive you—not necessarily for your sake, but for theirs.

Right now, your son or daughter probably wants to be closer to you than ever. Still, you might have to wait for an opportune time to discuss what's separated you. It's like awaiting your grandchild's birth, but, this time you'll be waiting for your child to come, full-term, into a forgiving reconciliation with you and a mature readiness for parenthood.

What can you do until then? How can you help your child be wellborn into parenting? Pray for his or her spiritual and mental health. Do what you can to encourage your son or daughter. And, if your child has wronged you or reflected badly on your parenting, now's a *grand* time to forgive!

Prayer: Dear Lord, help me and my family come fully before You, reflecting Your love and forgiveness in Christ's name.

Journey with God: Ask God to bring to your mind anything you need to forgive. Pray for a timely moment and appropriate words to seek your child's forgiveness and healing of your relationship.

____

____

____

____

____

____

____

____

Day 14

If the foot would say, "Because I am not a hand, I do not belong to the body," that would not make it any less a part of the body.

1 Corinthians 12:15, NRSV

In the preschool years, your son or daughter used to say, "Me do it!" which translated as, "I want to do it by myself!" Now that your child has a child, you might hear a slightly different version of the same message: "Thanks, Mom/Dad, but we're fine. We don't need any help with the baby—really!"

It's not that no one needs you anymore! You're not unwanted. Your son or daughter just prefers to be independent and grown-up, which are very responsible attitudes to have.

Most new parents want time alone with their baby to become familiar with their child and the new routines of parenthood. They also want to see if they're good at this job without anyone hovering over them! That's natural. That's normal. That's healthy. And that need not exclude you!

During these first few days of being a mom or dad, your child and his/her spouse probably could use some physical help—not with the baby so much as with daily chores. If you live near them or can take time from your home and work, they will be glad for household help.

The type of help you provide, however, won't just depend on them, but on you. For instance, if you're reasonably handy in the kitchen, you can cook their favorite meals. Or, put your feet to running errands. Shoulder the laundry; face that mound of dishes!

Whatever you do, though, do only what you can. Don't force yourself to fit into some part of your child's family that puts a squeeze on you or chafes them! Get started on the right foot, hand, shoulder, or any other part that lets you take part in this important stage of your child's life!

Prayer: Heavenly Father, thank You for giving family members what it takes to be supportive of one another. Please show me where my help best fits in Jesus' name.

Journey with God: In this journaling space, ask God about the type of help your child most needs right now.

____

____

____

____

____

____

____

____

Day 15

I am not concerned with great matters or with subjects too difficult for me. Instead, I am content and at peace. As a child lies quietly in its mother's arms, so my heart is quiet within me.

Psalm 131:1–2, TEV

As the new family adjusts to their first few days at home together, they'll need you to bring something special, something they probably haven't acquired yet for themselves—a calm, serene spirit!

At first, new parents don't trust their parenting instincts too much. They've had no opportunity yet to test them. So, whether you're near or far away, one of your first tasks as a grandparent will be to keep calm and let the new mother and father learn about their new job.

Staying unruffled and somewhat inconspicuous lets the novice mom and dad know that everything's fine. You give the new parents a chance to adjust to the demands of their newborn. You also help them to start trusting themselves to figure out, logically and lovingly, what their baby needs. They will! After all, you raised at least one of them!

If a crisis does occur, you'll be right there—on the spot or on the phone—to help. If your son or daughter asks a question, you'll answer what you know. In their home or yours, as you fold the laundry, scour a sink or feed the dog, your mind stays free and unperturbed to do *your* job—pray!

As you uplift family matters, great or small, to the Lord, you'll be satisfied—content—that you have done your most important work in helping this new household stabilize and adjust. You'll be at peace with your family and yourself, knowing that each of your concerns rests quietly with God.

Prayer: Heavenly Father, please quieten my spirit. Help me to trust You and my child to do a good job in Jesus' name.

Journey with God: Ask God to bring to your mind the prayers He wants you to pray for this new family.

Day 16

And thine ears shall hear a word behind thee, saying, This is the way, walk ye in it, when ye turn to the right hand, and when ye turn to the left.

Isaiah 30:21, KJV

"My, how times have changed!"

Remember that big, heavy pot you used to set on the stove top every time you sterilized baby bottles? Remember how the water took forever to come to a boil? Remember how very carefully—and perhaps awkwardly—you used tongs to remove the bottle rack? Then you let everything cool on clean dish towels, remember? Well, forget it!

Dishwashers and microwaves have changed all that. Now instead of pot watching, you can see if the scrub cycle ended or the microwave shut off. Or during the new family's first few days at home, you might not watch anything but a dwindling supply of premeasured, premixed, prepackaged bottles that you don't wash at all. You just toss them into a recycle bin!

How your child decides to do things depends on personal choice. As long as the bottles get cleaned and the germs get killed, the baby won't suffer. And, neither will your pride as you learn a new thing or two! But then, that's another part of grandparenting—being open to fresh discoveries.

As the grandparent, your *responsibilities* give way to *possibilities!* If your child and his or her spouse want to do something exactly as you would, fine. If they have another method in mind, that's also fine. Unless someone breaks one of the Ten Commandments, you don't need to wonder which way is right or wrong—just right or left! And that's more than fine! This way fine-tunes your ear to hear God *right* and to realize He has more *left* for you to do!

Prayer: Oh, Lord, what am I doing here? It's hard to stay calm when familiar ways seem tossed aside. I don't like to doubt my own judgment about even the smallest matters! Yet I want to listen and learn. Help me to hear what my child needs. Help me to hear what You want in Jesus' name.

Journey with God: Do you suspect you've been "set in your ways" a bit? Listen to the impressions God brings to your mind—thoughts that keep you flexible and attuned to Him.

Then describe what you hear.

____

____

____

____

____

____

____

Day 17

As the mountains surround Jerusalem, so the LORD surrounds his people, from this time on and forevermore.

Psalm 125:2, NRSV

Isn't feeding your grandbaby a snap? You just encircle the infant in your arms or on your lap and hold the bottle at a comfortable angle for you both.

Diaper changing is a snap too, especially if you use the smallest sized, form-fitting throwaways with sticky tabs.

However, if you stick around the new family for a while, you might be asked to bathe the baby! That can be a slippery task, but you can do it!

Just go slow, and take hold of your thoughts before you hold the baby. That umbilical cord needn't scare you. You know it will soon become a tummy button; then cleaning it will be a snap too! Meanwhile, you simply keep the area disinfected and dry—but you already remembered that.

For less than a second, you might think you've forgotten how to hold a newborn for sponge bathing. But long before a slight wobble scares you or your grandchild, you'll have the baby safely tucked into the cradle of your arm.

That's how God wants to hold you. Since your job is to let Him, don't squirm or pull away!

As you help your son or daughter and the new baby become accustomed to one another's wants and needs, your love—and, therefore, God's—will surround them. So, keep your family covered! Let God's love get a good hold on you!

Prayer: Heavenly Father, thank You for tending to my needs as I tend to my new grandchild. Help me to trust myself into the care of Your embrace. Help me to take hold of the love, power, and forgiveness I've found in Jesus' name.

Journey with God: Talk with God about each need you see in your family. If something looks as though it may take a while to cleanse, heal, or restore, note that situation in the space below. Make a prayer list to help you remember to hold these needs before God steadily in prayer.

Cry out for wisdom.
Beg for understanding.
Search for it as you would for silver.
Hunt for it like hidden treasure.
Then you will understand what it
means to respect the LORD.
Then you begin to know God.

Proverbs 2:3–4, NCV

"Mom/Dad, the baby just keeps crying, and I don't have any idea what's the matter. Do you?"

Until the new baby sounds more familiar, your son or daughter may want you to say what you think a particular cry means. If you know, by all means, tell! If not, just say so.

As you listen to various sounds the baby makes, you'll recognize some immediately. Sleepiness and stomach distress have fairly distinctive sounds, but often bigger clues come from the baby's accompanying gestures.

For instance, a yawn or a little fist rubbed against an eye illustrates a baby's tiredness. Flailing arms or legs can indicate an uncomfortable position or a chafing diaper. Knees drawn toward the chest can signal stomach pain from an empty tummy or one too full of food, air, or stomach gases.

Sometimes it's hard to tell if an infant wants food or has already had enough to cause discomfort. However, a clock and the baby will usually let you know! If it's been at least two hours since the last feeding, it may be time for another. If the baby refuses milk, it probably isn't time to eat, no matter what the clock says!

Although still an infant, your grandchild has already begun to develop a unique personality and voice. So, one baby won't sound exactly like the next. Yet each has the same basic needs, and each longs to have those needs met promptly! Sound familiar? Child or adult, everyone cries to be cared for and loved.

Prayer: Dear Lord, I really, really want Your wisdom and Your love! Without Your help, I have no help to give anyone—not even a tiny infant. Help me to understand my own heartfelt cries as I seek You in Jesus' name.

Journey with God: What makes you feel like crying? Thank God that He has always understood you and your needs. Ask Him to help you better understand cries for help within your family and within yourself.

How beautiful you are, my darling!
Oh, you are beautiful!

Song of Solomon 4:1, NCV

As surely as your grandchild awakens from a nap, crying to be held or fed, so will the child's mother awaken to new and troubling emotions. Your daughter or daughter-in-law, "out of the blue," may feel blue, yet these unpredictable moods are quite predictable! Some call them "baby blues." Others use the clinical term, postpartum depression, so labeled from the Latin *post* (follows) and *partum* (parturition or giving birth.)

Since the new mother's body and hormonal balance have to readjust to a nonpregnant state, mood shifts will naturally occur. Energy levels, depleted by labor and subsequent nights of inadequate rest, can make these mood shifts seem to swing wildly! Yet this, too, is "normal"—nothing to worry about—as long as no life-threatening danger exists.

Even under normal conditions, however, baby blues must not be ignored. Often they show a critical need for rest. Sometimes they indicate a physical, mental, or hormonal state that's unsafe for mother or child. Should such a condition exist, you might gently suggest seeking her doctor's counsel.

Usually, baby blues color the first days of parenting with grief. For nine months, the mother and child were one. Now parturition has parted them, and the new mother's body, mind, and spirit must adapt. If she's constantly tired from lack of sleep and depressed by her lack of experience or her looks, the adjustment can take longer or become dangerous.

To encourage a safe transition, you will of course continue to pray. You'll also provide grand help as you fully embrace the new mother with words of kindness, love, hope, and understanding. With God's help, tell her, often and well, how very lovely and very pleasing she is to you.

Prayer: Dear God, in Jesus' name, please help me remember to say and do those things that uplift, uphold, and embrace the new family, especially the new mother of my grandchild.

Journey with God: Ask God to bring to your mind what your daughter or daughter-in-law most needs to hear from you. Write those reminders here and review them before each visit with her.

____

____

____

____

____

____

I laid me down and slept;
I awaked;
for the LORD sustained me.

Psalm 3:5, KJV

"No one told me that parenting would be a twenty-four-hours-a-day, seven-days-a-week job! Will I ever have any time to myself again? Will I ever get some sleep?"

Having a new baby in the house does change everything!

When new parents first realize this, it's quite a shock. Most couples expected to make some adjustment in their schedules, but they had no idea they'd be on call all day, every day! Perhaps that wouldn't be so hard if they weren't on call all night, every night too!

No matter how young and energetic a new parent is, no one can keep going under those conditions. Moods will swing. Tears will erupt. Tempers will flare. Words will fly. And, if anyone has to go to work outside the home, frustration and fatigue will spill onto that job too!

If you can help the new family get some rest by staying overnight, fine. Or, perhaps you could ask the new parents if they would like for you to find a baby-sitter to sleep over or to give them an evening out by themselves. If so, you can pray for God to lead you to a reputable person who can be trusted to take care of the baby. If not, you can still pray!

Being physically present, losing sleep yourself, and/or trying to solve the new parents' problems are not your tasks as a grandparent! These belong to your child and his or her spouse. Yet around the clock, you're on call too! Night or day, you can pray about any and every situation that the Lord brings to your mind!

Prayer: Dear Father, please help my child and family rest in You. Bless their sleep, and give them the strength they need in Jesus' name.

Journey with God: Have you had trouble going to sleep lately? Ask God to help you rest in Him by bringing to your mind His prayer requests for this day or evening. Ask Him to help you know what specific gift of time you're to give your child.

____

____

____

____

____

____

____

____

____

Then Mary took a whole pint of a very expensive perfume made of pure nard, poured it on Jesus' feet, and wiped them with her hair. The sweet smell of the perfume filled the whole house.

John 12:3, TEV

Isn't your grandbaby the most adorable child you ever saw? Don't you just want to run out and buy every cute outfit and toy you can find? Don't you wish you could provide every advantage and fulfill every want or need your granddaughter or grandson could possibly have? But, don't most gifts seem to understated to show your overflowing love and joy?

Mary probably felt this dilemma too. She may have wondered, "What can I get Jesus? How can I show how much I adore Him?"

A common, everyday item just wouldn't do! She wanted to lavish adoration, profusely. So she bought perfume that cost more than most people earned in a year and dumped the whole bottle right on Jesus' feet! However, the perfume didn't stay there. Its fragrance permeated the whole house.

If you can afford an extravagant gift for your grandbaby and want to buy one, that's wonderful! But, just as Jesus said Mary's lavish act would always be remembered, so might yours! That's wonderful, too—assuming you've prayerfully considered the effect your gift will have on the whole house.

Will your purchase bring a good smell? Or will it seem—as Mary's did to Judas—odious? Jealousy, greed, rivalry, or misunderstandings about your motives can occur, especially if someone in your family feels left out or has other plans for your cash! So, bring your offerings and your gifts—aware and in prayer. Let your best gift be an outpouring of *pure* love.

Prayer: Dear God, I don't want to be caught up in anyone's self-centered attitudes—not even mine! I want to give good gifts, pleasing to You. Thank You for showing me I've nothing to be concerned about anytime I give from one motivation—love. Thank You for Your lavish outpouring of the pure and perfect gift of Your Son, Jesus.

Journey with God: As you journal, offer each gift idea to God and let Him reveal your motives in giving it.

"As bad as you are, you know how to give good things to your children. How much more, then, will your Father in heaven give good things to those who ask him!"

Matthew 7:11, TEV

Isn't it great? You don't have to spend a year's salary to buy a present for your grandchild! Love and attention to his or her needs will provide something that's indispensable. Since your grandbaby is too young to open packages, your gift giving mainly benefits your son or daughter who may or may not say what's wanted! You may hear hints, though, wrapped in phrases such as, "Oh, I wish we had . . ." or, "I've been meaning to get . . . ."

Maybe your child will come right out and say, "Yes! I'd really like ___!" But, if you don't have a clue about what's wanted or needed, consider giving a practical item that you haven't yet seen around the house.

For example, most parents need to transport their baby in a car, but state laws require safety-approved, protective infant carriers which can be fairly expensive.

Besides protecting their child, most young couples also want to guard the environment, but few have time to launder cloth diapers. To avoid disposable diapers (which, as it turns out, aren't too disposable after all) consider treating them (and future generations) to a diaper service.

As you think about the right gift, be observant, and you will hear or see what's needed. Don't worry that you'll be guilty of spoiling anyone! You know how to give good gifts. No matter how old your child and grandchild get, they will continue to need your love, attention, and prayers—good and priceless gifts that only you can give.

Prayer: Heavenly Father, thank You for the perfect gift of Your Holy Spirit at work in my family in the name, power, and love of Your Son, Jesus.

Journey with God: Look! Listen! Note the ways you have observed God's presence in your family. Have you ever been remiss about seeking forgiveness or refusing to accept God's love?

Confess those now.

____

____

____

____

____

____

____

____

____

____

Day 23

For the wages of sin is death; but the gift of God is eternal life through Jesus Christ our Lord.

Romans 6:23, KJV

Some gifts last an incredibly long time. Maybe you'll find a few, given years ago and now stored in your basement, garage, attic, or child's old bedroom. Those gifts have faded or seemed old and dirty, but they might be worth a closer look.

Is that a crib or cradle someone made for you or your baby? Did loving hands carve and paint a rocking horse or embroider tiny clothes? Isn't that the quilt or afghan you used to wrap up your own newborn so many years ago?

Memories weave a beautiful pattern into old blankets, clothes, toys, and baby furniture. As you see yellowed paint or loosened threads and smell a musty odor, you might be tempted to say, "Rubbish!" Perhaps they are. But some things can't be bought at the mall! Some things can't be replaced. Something made each item memorable to you too. Years ago you might have said, "Oh, don't throw that old thing away! It'll be worth a bundle when it's finally an antique. Then I'll sell it!" But, more likely, you kept it for sentimental value, and now it may mean something special to your child.

Since its condition has soiled over the years, naturally you don't want to expose a newborn to its layers of grime or germs. Soap and water or dry cleaning will work wonders! Just don't expect even the most superior cleaning methods to make anything really old become really new again.

As much as you love your family, you can't give them *perfectly* reconditioned antiques—or memories. Only God can fully restore anything. Only He can give what outlasts time and stays forever new. Only He can preserve true treasures and keep, for all eternity, your family and you.

Prayer: Dear Lord and Savior, please bring restoration and eternal life to my family in Jesus' name.

Journey with God: Think about what makes you and your family special because of what God restored or gave or preserved. Recall one special memory by writing it out below.

____

____

____

____

____

____

____

____

But now thus saith the LORD *that created thee, O Jacob, and he that formed thee, O Israel, Fear not: for I have redeemed thee, I have called thee by thy name; thou art mine.*

Isaiah 43:1, KJV

Have you told *everyone* about your new grandchild? Do your friends and church and other family members know your good news? When all goes well, you can enjoy the attention and congratulatory remarks, but you might also welcome the prayers of people who care about your family's concerns.

If your church publishes a newsletter or announces births in a weekly bulletin, call the office to have your good news included. Most hospitals notify newspapers in the city where new parents live, but if your son or daughter grew up in another town, you might notify that paper too.

Traditionally, grandparents can hardly wait to show off pictures and tell everyone they know about the birth of their grandson or granddaughter! But even in the "good ole days," that wasn't always true. Sometimes the "stork visited" an unwed mother's house, and no one wanted to mention it again. Those circumstances have increased so much, there's a strong possibility they include members of your church or your family. If so, you might feel confused about your role or status and even wonder, "Am I a grandparent or not?"

Regardless of your son or daughter's marital status, your grandchild still exists. You can acknowledge that life while making the details no one's business but yours! For example, in a hometown newspaper or your church newsletter, you might place this type of announcement: "Mr. and Mrs. ____ (your name) of ____ (town/state) announce the birth of their grandchild ___ (first and middle name) on ___ (date) to their son/daughter ___ (first name)."

Deserved or not, God redeems you. He calls you by His name. You can choose to do the same for your grandchild.

Prayer: Praise You, God, for Your good news in Jesus' name!

Journey with God: Even if your child is happily married you might feel embarrassed, upset, or confused about some other situation in your family. Ask God how you're to handle the announcement or details of your grandchild's birth.

____

____

____

____

____

____

____

One God and Father of all,
who is above all, and through all,
and in you all.

Ephesians 4:6, KJV

It's no one's business whether your grandchild's parents are married. But if not, have you consoled yourself with thoughts such as, *Well, Adam and Eve just lived together!*

People can only speculate, but apparently in Bible tradition, two people came to marriage by making vows to each other and to God. Then later, as civil laws arose, couples in most countries had to get a license before they could get married.

Although countries and states continue to recognize common law marriages, civil law makes marriage vows legal and binding. Otherwise, without this civic legality, any children born become known as "illegitimate," meaning they don't have the protection of certain *legal* rights they could otherwise *legitimately* claim.

Ironically, most churches and states agree that married couples aren't required to have a church wedding to have a *legal* marriage. Yet, couples married in churches receive certain *spiritual* rights as the church, authorized by Jesus Christ, pronounces a blessing on the marriage union.

Whether your grandchild has been born in wedlock or out, adopted, or produced by a second marriage, you can help protect this child—spiritually, legally, and lovingly too!

If, for example, no legal rights exist, you can have a new will drawn to be sure your grandbaby has a legitimate right to part of your estate. If the church hasn't been given an opportunity to bless the family, you can draw on God's will in constant prayer, interceding on behalf of this child. You can pray for God's spiritual protection over your family as He helps each person come to accept Him and believe.

Prayer: Dear God and Father of all, thank You for being in my life. Please draw my family to Your will in Jesus' name.

Journey with God: Talk with God about any legitimate concerns you have for this grandchild. Offer illegitimate worries to Him too! Record them in the columns below.

Legitimate Concerns	Illegitimate Worries

"We cannot keep quiet. We must speak about what we have seen and heard."

Acts 4:20, NCV

"I don't know what's the matter with me lately. The last thing I want to do is hurt my child, but I just can't seem to keep my mouth shut!"

One of the responsibilities of parenting involves your willingness to correct something you see that isn't right. Although your child has grown up, that doesn't mean he or she has grown into complete maturity or perfection!

In an effort to be quiet about areas that still need correction, some parents clamp their lips shut, yet their actions betray their thoughts or feelings. Or, they might approach a subject in a roundabout way, dropping hints and innuendoes, thinking they have no right to say anything outright.

If something troubles you, there's nothing wrong with saying so! Most parents just don't want to risk confronting or losing a child who turns away from their correction. Most also realize that their grown children have rights too, including the freedom to make mistakes. But some parents create or add to mistakes by a harsh, unloving tone which says, "As far as I'm concerned, *nothing* you do will *ever* be right!"

In these first days of parenting, your son or daughter has many adjustments to make. Some changes might bring about the very things you have been wanting to see anyway!

But, as you stay in contact with the new family, don't keep quiet about anything you see that's right! Focus your eyes and thoughts on what's commendable and favorable about their parenting skills. When you cannot help but speak of what you've seen and heard, state well your overflowing love, good news, and glowing report!

Prayer: Dear God, please help me be slow to comment about anything my child does wrong as I wait for You to show me the right time and place for correction. Help me be quick to see, hear, and speak of the good in my family in Christ's name.

Journey with God: Write down what you see and hear from God about His goodness in your child and family.

But now in Christ Jesus you who once were far off have been brought near by the blood of Christ.

Ephesians 2:13, NRSV

Remember the story, "The Prodigal Son"? Jesus didn't title it that. Other people did. In His parable, the story did not center around the son. It focused on a *parent* and his forgiving love, not just for one son—for two!

To paraphrase: one wayward son takes his inheritance and splits! Waking up in a pigpen brings him to his senses, so he goes home. Immediately, his dad (who'd apparently been on the lookout, waiting) spots him and races to greet his son—a young man who still hasn't proven he values his heritage or plans to embrace family tradition! This son has not helped out, behaved responsibly, or done anything but show up!

Meanwhile, the older son sees what's going on, hears plans for a celebration, and starts to stew! He's been dutiful and dependable his whole life. He's always helped. He's never done anything to shame his family. Yet his self-seeking sibling gets a returning hero's welcome! The older brother doesn't intend to dishonor his father, but he's certainly NOT going to honor his father's younger son!

While this elder child is *still far off* from a reconciliation with his brother—and *still far off* from enjoying the celebration—he experiences exactly what his younger brother did.

He loses all closeness with his family. Yet, once again, the father recognizes the pain of a wayward heart, and his love draws still another child home.

As you celebrate the coming of your grandchild, other family members may seem to pull away. That's to be expected as everyone adjusts to this change. Yet no one needs to go too far from your reminder, "I love you. I'm glad you're here!"

Prayer: Oh, most merciful Father, I know I've drawn away from You, just as my child sometimes seems distant from me. Thank You for Jesus' love which enables us to live near You always.

Journey with God: Ask God how He wants you to encourage and celebrate your family's closeness to each other and to Him. Plan one way to demonstrate this sense of celebration to your family.

The LORD appeared to him from far away. I have loved you with an everlasting love; therefore I have continued my faithfulness to you. Again I will build you, and you shall be built.

Jeremiah 31:3–4, NRSV

If your son or daughter lives nearby, you'll probably have many opportunities to become close to your grandchild. However, these first days of grandparenting bring a unique time to ensure future closeness as you begin now to establish a bond.

Holding the baby so he or she can hear your heartbeat and voice helps your grandson or granddaughter develop an early attachment to you. As you delight in the soft skin, sweet smell, and adorable infant in your arms, you'll find your affections deepening too.

Early bonding begins a loving support system that helps a child to flourish in the growing up years and continues to provide a stabilizing influence throughout life. If you're far away, you'll naturally want to visit as soon and as often as you can. Yet, from a distance—and from your own home—you can still find ways to draw near.

For instance, when you telephone to check on everyone, ask your child to place the receiver near the baby's ear. Call his or her name and say, "I love you. I'm glad you were born." Add other words of welcome as they come to you. Between calls, record a message, song or prayer, and send the cassette to be played in the nursery.

Throughout your day—and through the years—draw close to your family by praying for them regularly. Ask God to help you faithfully show His everlasting love. Ask Him to help you create healthy bonds and build up each family member, no matter how very far away a person seems.

Prayer: Dear Father, thank You for Your bond of everlasting love that faithfully draws my family to You in Jesus' name.

Journey with God: Write down the ways you feel God wants you to strengthen family ties or build a healthy support system for each family member.

Give ear to my prayer, O God;
and hide not thyself
from my supplication.
Attend unto me, and hear me:
I mourn in my complaint,
and make a noise.

Psalm 55:1–2, KJV

Has your son or daughter asked you to baby-sit? If you enjoy the company of infants, you'll be delighted to have your new grandson or granddaughter all to yourself! You'll treasure these special times together. But, if you're baffled by babies and the mystifying noises they make, you might feel like hiding from the request!

No matter what you ask of God, He does not hide Himself from you! He gives His whole attention to your questions, petitions, problems, and appeals. Therefore, you can *decide* to follow His example, and do the same for your child.

It may not be easy. You may have a complaint. Yet, you can listen to each request and give it your full attention. This doesn't mean an automatic "yes!" It just means you will not draw back from listening. You'll hear and consider what your son or daughter has to say. Then, if you can oblige, you will. If you can't, you won't. It's that simple—usually!

Sometimes, what's asked is not at all what's being said! For example, you may hear, "Can you come stay with the baby a few minutes while I run to the store?" Since it's probably just as easy for you to do the shopping, the request might mean, "I really need a break!" But that's harder to admit!

As you prayerfully listen to a request, consider who's asking. If, for instance, your child calls you all the time, he or she may need extra encouragement such as, "You're doing fine!" Or, if your son or daughter doesn't like to ask anyone for anything, the request may be very important. But don't wonder! Ask God, and, yes or no, *He will answer your request!*

Prayer: Dear Father, I want my child to let me know when help is needed. Please remind me to come to You when I need help in Jesus' name.

Journey with God: Ask God to bring to your mind any requests from your child that you didn't hear or have left unanswered. Listen as He also brings to mind the answer you're to give. Record your insights here.

____

____

____

____

____

____

____

____

Ask, and it shall be given you; seek, and ye shall find; knock, and it shall be opened unto you.

Matthew 7:7, KJV

Does your child often *ask* for favors? Does he or she frequently drop by uninvited to *seek* your free time, a free meal, free advice, or a few dollars that probably won't be repaid? Does he or she *knock* your lifestyle, choices, habits, or personality, opening old resentments or wounds?

If you have a child who keeps *asking* you to do this or that, sooner or later you'll do it just to keep from hearing about it anymore! If you have a child who keeps *seeking* your help, you'll probably give it. If you have one who keeps *knocking* your way of life, you'll eventually realize, "Boy, do I feel used!"

If you've ever been in such situations, you know that what you want is a way to open the lines of communication between your child and yourself about each other's needs and expectations, but start by *asking* how *you* feel about each request or expectation your family places on you. *Seek* information about your use of time, energy and money. If you feel *knocked* around by the demands of others, be *open* to another response than your typical one.

Take, for example, your time. Do you feel you never have enough to do what's needed? If so, how does that make you feel? And how do you feel when your child adds to that stress by wanting or expecting more help? What can you do to alleviate the demands placed on you—or ones you place on yourself? Do you expect too much from yourself? Do others?

Find out. Ask God for His viewpoint. Seek His priorities for you. Keep on knocking away until you find the truth. Then *be open* to acting on the information God reveals to you.

Prayer: Dear God, I want to be there for my family, but not every second of every day! Please help me to remember to ask You about what You want me to do. Help me to seek Your will before distributing the time, energy, and money You've given me to use in Jesus' name.

Journey with God: Has "being there" for your family made you feel "beside yourself" or away from God? Listen to what He expects from you and how He wants you to handle each situation that arises.

For we are what he has made us, created in Christ Jesus for good works, which God prepared beforehand to be our way of life.

Ephesians 2:10, NRSV

When you were a child, did your grandparents seem, well, ancient? Did their way of life mean sitting on the porch in a rocking chair playing peek-a-boo with the newest baby? Does your child now want you to "act like a grandparent" too?

If being a grandparent makes you feel incredibly old, it's probably time to get off the porch! Or, if you've been racing around, running errands and doing jobs for everyone in the family, you might already be off your rocker! You might be trying to meet your child's expectations in an effort to avoid your own antiquated view.

Before you adjust to changing roles, you need some idea of what grandparenting means. Ironically, it has little to do with age, yet you're suddenly, and perhaps, painfully aware that you're not twenty! You probably haven't been for a few years, but neither are you past the century mark. You're not as young as you were, but neither are you as old as you feel!

Primarily, your changing role means you're not the new parent of the new baby. Your child has that responsibility now. You can help, but you can also get a good night's sleep! You no longer have to plan your schedule or center your activities around a newborn. You can hold, diaper, and yes, rock the baby! But when he or she wails, you can give the child back to his or her parents!

Being a grandparent brings changes, but it has advantages too. So, as you alter the outdated views of grandparenting you and your child have, reconsider your way of life. Let your newly emerging role be created in Christ for the good work God has now given you to do!

Prayer: Lord, please give me Your view of grandparenting in Jesus' name.

Journey with God: Do you or your child expect you to behave a certain way now that you're a grandparent? Ask God to reveal His expectations. Record them here and then plan a time to talk about them with your child.

____

____

____

____

____

____

____

____

Day 32

[Jesus said,] "Earthly food spoils and ruins. So don't work to get that kind of food. But work to get the food that stays good always and gives you eternal life. The Son of Man will give you that food. God the Father has shown that He is with the Son of Man."

John 6:27, NCV

"You're spoiling that child to death!" Has anyone said that to you? If so, you might be wondering if they're right! Jesus once talked of spoilage in familiar terms everyone understood—food!

When vegetables, fruit, and meat become spoiled, they're useless and not much good for anything because their main purpose—to feed and nourish—has been thwarted. Likewise, if children grow up with no aim except to demand, "Give me! Gimme!" their usefulness or fruitfulness may diminish or die too.

Food also spoils through mishandling: rough treatment bruises. Neglect brings leanness. As the plants grow, too much or too little protection decreases their overall strength and inhibits their growth. Poor stakes (goals) and weak stems (motives) send growth in the wrong direction.

Eventually, the best-grown produce will do its job well and be gone. But, unlike food meant for consumption, people bear fruit in both mind and spirit. Physically, a person's shape, size, color, form, weight, and energy won't stay the same, but in Christ, well-nourished minds and spirits last forever.

The next time you fear spoiling your child or grandchild to death, ask if you're doing anything to squeeze, bruise, or crush their soul. Probably not! But do question the long-term spiritual value of your actions. Also, remember: Only Christ has pure, unblemished food for the spirit. Only He can nurture your family with unspoiled love that lasts forever.

Prayer: Dear Father, I don't want to spoil Your plans for my family's physical, mental, or spiritual growth. I don't want to thwart what You've created. Help my love be purified and empowered by the Holy name and Spirit of Jesus Christ.

Journey with God: Ask God if your human kindness has spoiled or delayed healthy growth in your child. Ask Him to bring to mind the work He's given you to do—work that nurtures the mental, physical, and spiritual development of your family.

____

____

____

____

____

____

____

The people asked Jesus, "What are the things God wants us to do?" Jesus answered, "The work God wants you to do is this: to believe in the One that God sent."

John 6:28–29, NCV

"I can't change what's happened! Everything seems hopeless!" Maybe that's how you're feeling, especially if you suspect you've spoiled a child or two! It's not that your parenting choices were all wrong, but having unproductive thoughts now won't do anything to straighten what's gone awry.

Even if your child turned out reasonably well and has already shown excellent parenting skills, there's a strong possibility you're not pleased with *everything* you've done or neglected to do. As you adapt to your changing role—from parent to grandparent—you might want to hurry up and fix everything you see!

Instead of working feverishly to change your family or yourself, consider the true work God gave you to do: believe the One He sent. That sounds simple, but, when faith ebbs and discouragement sets in, the work of faith becomes hard labor.

Believing in the One God sent means you have faith, not in yourself, but in Christ. In Him, nothing stays hopeless forever. He has the power to save—and to keep on mending!

As you believe in the One God sent, your growing faith strengthens you and your family too. God gave you a child, and you became a parent. So ap*PARENT* ly, God has faith in you! He continues to show that faith by giving your child a child.

So, believe it! Believe that God knows what He's doing! Believe in His power, ability, and willingness to work out problems. And when a situation seems hopeless or intolerable, just put your faith to work! *Believe* in the One God sent.

Prayer: Dear God, help my unbelief! Forgive me for letting my faith go slack when it's most needed. Thank You for Jesus—the One You sent to help us always.

Journey with God: What chronic, worrisome or hopeless situation do you face as a parent or grandparent? Write a prayer below and ask God how you're to put your faith in Him to work in that situation.

____

____

____

____

____

____

____

Day 34

For I the LORD your God am a jealous God, punishing children for the iniquity of parents, to the third and fourth generation of those who reject me, but showing steadfast love to the thousandth generation of those who love me and keep my commandments.

Exodus 20:5–6, NRSV

Not too many parents like to think they've ruined a child or grandchild! It's much easier to blame someone or something else. For instance, your grandparents might have mentioned "bad blood," or your parents might have talked about "history repeating itself." Maybe you've thought in terms of a poor environment or bad genes.

Regardless of the terminology, most people agree that one generation passes certain physical, mental, and spiritual characteristics to the next. Frankly, that's depressing—not to mention hopeless! Who can change their past environment or alter their upbringing? Who can correct a family's blood, history, genetic pool or whatever you want to call it?

God calls this problem "iniquity" or "sin." His Word clearly identifies the problem and warns about sins of the fathers (which includes mothers)! Three or four generations will feel the unfavorable effects of those sins, but what's worse, each generation might continue to perpetuate them and the problem!

The situation sounds incurable, the damage irreparable. It is—unless someone accepts responsibility! Someone must love God enough and believe in Him enough to trust

Him. Someone must finally stop saying, "My parents did that," and rather say "*I* did it!"

Confession breaks sin's cycle and brings the solution. By loving and obeying God, you receive His promise of love for at least a thousand generations—starting now with you!

Prayer: God, I'd much rather blame my parents, grandparents, or society than myself! I don't like some characteristics that keep coming up again and again in my family. I didn't choose them, but I don't choose to perpetuate them either! I admit to You my failure and my sin. I accept responsibility for the mistakes I've made, and ask for Your forgiveness in the untarnished name of Your Son, Jesus.

Journey with God: Ask God to bring to mind anything you need to confess. Offer that to Him. Then describe your experience of forgiveness.

____

____

____

____

____

____

____

____

Be ye therefore merciful, as your Father also is merciful. Judge not, and ye shall not be judged: condemn not, and ye shall not be condemned: forgive, and ye shall be forgiven.

Luke 6:36–37, KJV

"It's just not fair! I didn't repeat *all* of my ancestor's mistakes, but I'm still affected by their failures, faults, and blunders!" No doubt you are. Your child probably is too. So, what can you do about it?

As you face the sins of your forefathers or foremothers, you have a couple of choices to make: (1) You can choose to perpetuate those very same sins every time you recall them to memory or (2) you can choose to be merciful and forgive.

Recollecting past mistakes—your own or someone else's—keeps a collection going for future generations to despise or enjoy! But collecting stamps of approval or disapproval doesn't help anyone. It fastens ancestors *and* descendants to a fixed wall of judgment and condemnation.

If you're like every other person on earth, generations of debris have been handed down to you. Like *everyone* else (including *your* parents, grandparents, and other relatives) you didn't have a choice about the rubbish you've acquired!

But, as with any other inheritance, *you get to decide* whether to hold onto the entire collection you've been given! Or you can mercifully choose to let go by choosing to forgive.

Maybe you'll feel better immediately. Maybe you won't! But feelings don't make the difference or the choice! Love for God and family helps you choose what's best. So close the books on old accounts of sin! Slam shut those archives, and choose to hang onto your memorable collection of God's love.

Prayer: Dear God, thank You for the forgiveness that You've mercifully shown me. I choose to hand it down to my family by first handing it back to the generations who have gone before me in Christ's name.

Journey with God: Think about the dual meaning of the word, *refuse*. It can mean to reject or decide against; it can also mean discarded material or trash. Confess any areas of unforgiveness. Refuse them as part of your family's heritage, and turn over the refuse of the past to God.

Day 36

Let this be recorded for a generation to come, so that a people yet unborn may praise the LORD.

Psalm 102:18, NRSV

Everything you've been handed wasn't meant to be thrown away! Some things are worth keeping.

As you sort through the memories and memorabilia you've kept in your attic (mind), garage (heart), or basement (subconscious), toss out old relics of the past that have shown themselves to be harmful. But retain what's worthy to be passed to future generations.

Consider your family's history, especially looking for reminders of the love and kindness your relatives have given to you over the years. Sort through fond memories and memorable stories that you prize. Not only will you be strengthened by these signs of your family's love, your child and grandchild will eventually be edified by them too.

In this mobile society, many families have scattered around the country. Many people lack family ties and roots. Few know enough *relatives* to find ones with whom they *relate!* So, instead of belonging everywhere they go, people feel as though they belong nowhere.

Regardless of your family's past or future, you have a history that your child and grandchild need to hear. Record it on tape if you like, or write it down. But do tell the interesting, inspiring, and courageous stories about your ancestors.

Note the faith passed from one generation to another. Document every new and wondrous account of God's work in your family's life. Help your descendants—born and unborn—learn to praise the Lord.

Prayer: Heavenly Father, thank You for redeeming my family and my record-keeping in Jesus' name.

Journey with God: Ask God to bring to your mind the stories and accounts He'd like you to remember and pass on. Ask for an awareness of His healing word and actions in your family.

Record one such story here before this day ends.

Now unto him that is able to keep you from falling, and to present you faultless before the presence of his glory with exceeding joy, To the only wise God our Saviour be glory and majesty, dominion and power, both now and ever. Amen.

Jude 24, KJV

Don't you just love having your picture taken? If you peer at old family photographs, most of your relatives probably look as though they weren't too thrilled with cameras either! However, they did go through the process which, in their day, may have been rather tedious. Without smiling or flinching, they presented themselves, dutifully, for descendants to see.

Looking at those faces now, you and your child can get to know them better. Eventually, your grandchild can too. As you bring out an old album or portrait, you'll tell your son or daughter what you know about that person. Or, perhaps your child will recall some story or memory to tell you.

When pictures pass from hand to hand, they become a visual illustration of your family's history. Although you probably won't part with your originals, notice the pictures which seem to mean the most to your child. Consider having additional prints made professionally, or make them yourself by photographing the photographs at close range.

On the lower back corner of each print, pencil in the date, place, occasion, and approximate year, along with the person's relationship and full name. That way family members will always be able to tell whose handsome faces they see!

Few relatives will look as good in a photograph as they did in person! But don't let that stop you from having your picture taken, particularly during family gatherings or group scenes. With Christ's love showing through you, you'll become highly presentable for future generations to see!

Prayer: Oh, Lord, some of my relatives look like characters! I'm not too sure I want my great-great-great-grandchildren snickering over my clothes or hair, but I do want to try to make myself known to them. Help me always to be seen as one who lives in the glory, power, and dominion of Christ's name.

Journey with God: So what's wrong with how you look? Discuss your physical, mental, and spiritual appearance with God.

____

____

____

____

____

____

____

____

For with you is the fountain of life;
in your light we see light.
Psalm 36:9, NRSV

Isn't your grandbaby the most adorable and photogenic child you ever saw? Naturally, you'll want lots of pictures to remind you of how very cute he or she looks and acts at various stages, growing up.

Natural, unposed poses provide memorable pictures. For instance, your grandchild can't yet get around alone, so now is just naturally the time to include each family member who holds the baby. Of course, that means you will occasionally need to hand the camera to someone to take your picture too!

In the coming years, these photographs will give your grandchild a reminder of relatives and how they related to him or her. So attempt to put everyone in a favorable light! Focus on the baby as you show each person hugging, rocking, kissing, playing with, or smiling at your grandchild.

Take several frames of each scene so you'll have plenty of pictures from which to choose. Then, if someone grimaces, suddenly moves, or looks perfectly awful, you can throw those unflattering photos away. Don't hold that pose forever!

To have picture perfect photographs with good contrast

and sharp focus, you'll need ample light. Without sufficient lighting, there's no picture at all. The whole scene becomes lost in darkness as though it never existed. However, a flash of too much light can startle a baby and, on close-ups, hurt those highly sensitive eyes.

Unless you're on a dark Damascus Road, headed away from God's will, the light of Christ will not hurt your eyes—or your feelings! Gently, lovingly, His light brings a clearer picture of yourself and family into view to help you develop more fully. You'll see! In light of His will, you will see.

Prayer: Lord, thank You for Your beautiful picture of me and my family, revealed in the loving light of Christ.

Journey with God: Has God brought into focus a habit, choice, or relationship that He wants you to see more clearly? Ask Him to help you see this matter in light of His will.

All of you are people who belong to the light, who belong to the day. We do not belong to the night or to the darkness.

1 Thessalonians 5:5, TEV

Now that you have such a terrific collection of baby pictures and family photos, you might want to start an album or scrapbook for your grandchild. If your son or daughter doesn't have the time or inclination to keep a baby book, you might consider doing that too.

As almost any writer can tell you, a well-done book contains three main ingredients: *a topic, a theme, and a purpose.* The baby book, scrapbook, or photograph album can easily contain all three.

- It will have a topic: your grandchild.
- It will have a theme: the child's life, primarily during the growing up years.
- It will have a purpose: to remind this child that he or she is loved.

Because you're a Christian, you'll want a little more light on this subject: the light of Christ! So, your topic becomes your grandchild shown in that light. The theme of the baby book or photo album focuses on your grandchild's life in Christ. Your purpose reveals the love of Christ.

Get the picture? Well, put yourself in it too! With or without photographs to illustrate, write down how you felt when you first saw your grandchild. Note the place and date your grandbaby first came to visit you. Record the first time you took your grandson or granddaughter to church, and tell what else happened that day.

Because you're in Christ, you belong to Him. His light belongs to you—it can't help but shine some on your family! So, from the start of your grandchild's life, you can show you belong to the day, the most important day when the Lord Jesus Christ makes Himself known, personally and individually, to every one of you!

Prayer: Oh, Lord, I do want You to be Lord of my life and my family! Please help me to reflect Your light to my grandbaby and each relative in Christ's name.

Journey with God: What picture do you have of your family—surrounded by spiritual darkness or enveloped in lightness and levity? Pray about dark areas, and ask God if you need to lighten up!

____

____

____

____

____

____

____

____

Day 40

Take delight in the LORD,
and he will give you the desires
of your heart.

Psalm 37:4, NRSV

Do you know of any allergies in your family? These can come to light when someone reacts badly to certain foods, such as citrus, wheat, seafood, or nuts, perhaps developing a headache, stomachache, fever, hives, or even nausea because of what they've eaten. Others may react to irritants in the air, sneezing or having difficulty breathing around cats, dogs, perfume, or fresh-cut flowers.

Dander, dust, pollen, sprays, preservatives, artificial sweeteners, chlorinated water and smoke from burning trash or cooking over an outdoor grill—any or all of these can cause mild or violent allergic reactions! If you've seen such problems on either side of the family, notify your child of the potential allergens that may some day affect your grandchild.

For instance, a family allergy to pecans doesn't seem significant until your grandchild is old enough to eat them. However, if your daughter or daughter-in-law eats pecan pie before breastfeeding, the baby could have a reaction. Or, if perfume gives someone in the family a severe headache, your child needs to know this before taking the baby out to visit. By identifying common allergens on both sides of the family, you help your child to better track them and any effects they may cause.

You may also see the need to handle certain matters differently yourself. For example, if your son or daughter has an allergic reaction every time you mention going to church, you might drop that subject for a while!

In varying degrees, allergic reactions indicate, "I can't tolerate this!" Even if your child is reacting badly to spiritual allergens, remember that you can take delight in the Lord! Feed on His Word. Breathe in His Spirit. Take personal joy in Him and His church. In time, reactions might settle down so everyone can "joy-in" you!

Prayer: Dear Lord, please forgive me for being hard to take sometimes. Help my family forgive me for pushing too much or too soon. I want to be taken with You and Your will, not mine. Help me to join Your joy in Jesus' name.

Journey with God: Is your child's response to church hard for *you* to take? Talk about it with God. Ask Him to help you see His delightful timing and to know *He also wants* what you desire!

____

____

____

____

____

One generation shall praise thy works to another, and shall declare thy mighty acts.

Psalm 145:4, KJV

"Oh, no! Don't make me drink that stuff!" If your child ever complained a lot about having to drink milk, he or she may have lactose intolerance. Now, your grandchild might show signs of being allergic to milk by spitting up frequently or having a sour odor right after taking a bottle. Since a baby must have milk, a soybean formula might provide immediate relief.

But other allergies can often be avoided by waiting to introduce a potential allergen until the child is three or four. For example, if family members suffer from hay fever, just be sure not to have any pollen-producing plants, flowers, or haystacks in your house!

Many allergies develop from intense exposure to or a heavy concentration of an irritant. In a similar way, well-meaning parents can luxuriate in a religious atmosphere that seems too heady or even toxic to their child. Ironically, if they "come on too strong," the person most likely to develop a spiritual allergic reaction is the very one who has a sensitive spirit.

In the medical community, a common method of treatment advocates massive doses or injections of the allergen. The end result accomplishes desensitization. Instead of reacting strongly, the person then does not react at all. So, if you feel concerned about your child's reaction to God, the Bible, or church, thank God for the sensitivity that's still apparent!

Prayerfully, wait for an opportune moment—a nontoxic time—to mention God in a natural or conversational way. This takes the focus from your child and his or her choices, and lets you direct the attention where it belongs—toward God's goodness and what He's done for you.

Prayer: Lord, help me to drink Your goodness without spilling a drop! Help me to stop saying what my family *should* do and speak pleasantly of what *You* do in Jesus' blessed name.

Journey with God: Do you see God's mighty acts around you? Do you see His work in your life? Ask God to bring to your mind everything that's worthy of your praise. List everything that comes to you.

____

____

____

____

____

____

____

The LORD is my chosen portion
and my cup; you uphold my lot.
My boundary lines have fallen for me
in pleasant places;
I have a goodly heritage.

Psalm 16:5–6, NRSV

As you drink in God's goodness, you'll be refreshed by His love, generously given to you and your family. If this tastes new, perhaps you'll be satisfied with an occasional sip! But you may want to gulp down every word of God's Word until you're filled to overflowing.

By seeing yourself in biblical context, you savor your place in the family of Christ. You nourish your faith. You learn more of your Christian heritage. You come to accept God's ample, ongoing, and personal provisions more fully. You see your true lot in life as a wonderful inheritance within the unlimited boundaries of God's love.

It's like getting a piece of property that someone has willed to you. Naturally, you would want to see for yourself what it's like, to decide for yourself if it's worth keeping.

The same holds true for your godly heritage. As you check it out, you see for yourself how God's will covers you with His love. You see how each Bible promise is meant for you to claim as your own. You see how each gift of the Holy Spirit has some impact on your life. You see how God's Word, will, and ways apply to your unique situation.

Now, you have something valuable to give! Now, you have a personal testimony! Now, you have a Christian perspective on what you know, see, hear, feel, and taste of God in your life. Now, you can be a credible witness in your family—one who personally attests to God's good gifts. Now, you have something to pass on.

Prayer: Dear Lord, please help me to see for myself the good inheritance You've given me and to pass it on in Jesus' name.

Journey with God: Are you willing to let your child and his or her family discover God's goodness for themselves? Discuss your fears and feelings with God.

I remember the days of old, I think about all your deeds, I meditate on the works of your hands.

Psalm 143:5, NRSV

Be honest. Does God *really* make a difference in your life? If so, what is it? Think about it. Meditate on it, and especially, remember.

Remember that time you didn't know what you would do to take care of your family? You needed lots of time, energy, money, or ______ (fill in the blank). But you didn't have any! So, you did the only thing you could do—pray. You trusted God and waited, expecting *something* to happen, even if it wasn't much!

When something did happen, you could hardly believe it! For a minute, you forgot you prayed. Perhaps you even started to think you'd worked things out by yourself! Yet something helped you to remember, and you knew: God had answered. God had done this. In exactly the right time, place, and way, God supplied everything you needed.

Over the years, other needs arose. Your family's life went on. Your child grew up and had a child. Although you never forgot God, you occasionally had trouble recalling what He'd done for you. Sometimes you couldn't see that He'd done much of anything! But looking back now, you know without a doubt: God has *always* been at work in your family.

Don't assume your child remembers everything! Tell your son or daughter and, eventually, your grandchild the difference God has made in your life. Tell why you're a Christian. Tell why you believe. Be specific. Give details! If no one wants to listen yet, put it in writing! Sooner or later, your words will be available to upbuild and encourage your family's faith.

Prayer: Dear God, help me to recall and note Your goodness in my life in Jesus' name.

Journey with God: Ask God to help you remember the prayers He has answered and works He has done to recall your family to Him.

I will sing a new song unto thee, O God: upon a psaltery and an instrument of ten strings will I sing praises unto thee.

Psalm 144:9, KJV

If you like to sing, you don't necessarily have to *tell* your child and grandchild about God. Sing about Him! Sing psalms and modern hymns. Sing about His mighty acts and His great love. Sing His name. Sing alleluia! Sing on key if you can, but, if not, don't let that stop your music!

Especially sing new songs—ones you make up yourself as you lyrically note your story or personal praise. Sing bright, uplifting, encouraging, joyous songs of God's love—songs that include each member of your family by name.

Right now, of course, your grandchild is much too young to understand the words, but that just gives you more time to practice! Meanwhile, the baby can feel the comfort of your attention, love, and reasonably calming tune. Your child may also be pleasantly affected—whether that's admitted or not!

Too often, windy sermons, erroneous teaching, hypocrisy, and unkind words from Christians of all ages have stopped young adults from churchgoing. However, that doesn't mean they have turned their backs on God! Sometimes, music is just the thing to help them recognize this difference.

A Christian recently recalled, "Growing up, I felt scorched in church! It sounded like everyone was going to hell, so I was afraid I would too if I stuck around! After a few years, I went back—to another denomination. But I kept seeking God because of a song I used to hear in Sunday School. I couldn't have been more than three or four when I first heard the lyrics, but I *believed* them. Even as a young child I knew: 'Jesus loves ME!' Now, this I know: It's true!"

Prayer: Oh God, help me to sing Your praise in such a simple, truthful, pleasant way that the people I love can hear and praise You too.

Journey with God: How do you *know* Jesus loves you? Think of the ways God has personally tried to teach you those lyrics. List any Christian songs or hymns that are particularly meaningful to you, convincing you of Jesus' love.

____

____

____

____

____

____

____

Day 45

For as the body is one, and hath many members, and all the members of that one body, being many, are one body: so also is Christ.

1 Corinthians 12:12, KJV

"Hey, everybody! It's time to get ready for church."

When your son or daughter was small, that's all you had to say, and, fast or slow, your family headed toward a time and place of worship. As your child reached the teen years, you had to speak a little louder or longer, but if you were determined, you probably got the results you wanted!

Now, everything has changed. You can do nothing to make your child go to church. Even if his or her family goes on their own, you have no say about which denomination they favor! If their choice happens to have a theological stance you question, you may feel tempted to get into a long-term wrestling match!

Instead of a family scuffle, prayerfully wrestle with these questions: Has my child turned his or her back on Jesus Christ? If so, the conflict isn't with your child but with the power of darkness, trying to draw him or her away. Has my son or daughter often expressed dissatisfaction with my denominational choice? If so, he or she may have said things like, "I don't fit in," or "I don't see it that way."

As you seek answers, you'll have light on how to pray, but the big question is: Does this child attend a church that proclaims Jesus Christ as Lord and Savior? If so, rejoice!

Even if you don't agree with the theology, you can accept the denominational differences as though they're different parts of Christ's body, varied according to their unique and separate functions, but each needed within Christ's body, Christ's bride, Christ's church.

Prayer: Dear God, I just want my family together! When we aren't, I'm disappointed. But I guess You're not too pleased when Your children bicker about their beliefs—especially if those beliefs happen to be about You! I'm sorry, Lord. Help me to accept my child's choice in Jesus' name.

Journey with God: Do you ever have trouble seeing someone else's point of view? Ask to see Christ's view of His body.

There is one body, and one Spirit, even as ye are called in one hope of your calling; One Lord, one faith, one baptism.

Ephesians 4:4–5, KJV

Did your child change churches so that he or she could attend services with a spouse? If so, that's probably where the couple will now take your grandchild! Perhaps they're already talking about a religious ceremony in that church, and you're not sure if you should even show up!

Think about it. Pray about it. Clarify the real issue as you ask yourself this very important question, "Do I want my grandchild to be dedicated to Christ?" Of course you do! Therefore, you can show your support of that decision by being there for the service—even if you feel uncomfortable with its format or style.

If, for example, you're from an evangelical church, you may feel upset if your infant grandchild is baptized. This isn't new! Jewish babies, like Jesus, were part of their faith by being born into it. However, at a later time (usually 12 or 13), they made a personal choice. In Christian churches which practice infant baptism, the child will also choose. Preteens, teens, or adults *confirm* a parent's choice at a time called *confirmation*.

If you're from a liturgical church, you may feel upset if your grandbaby isn't baptized now. Eventually, the child will have that choice. Meanwhile, a dedication service has a similar purpose as parents come before the Lord, vowing to do what they can to provide a Christ-centered home.

Whether you participate in a dedication ceremony or an infant baptismal service, you can take your rightful place in the body of Christ. You have the right—as a Christian and a grandparent—to make this commitment! Sincerely vow to do all you can to upbring your grandchild to the Lord.

Prayer: Dear Lord, help me to accept the whole body of Christ and remain part of it in His name.

Journey with God: Does your child know how you feel about his or her denominational choice? Ask to hear God's word before you speak. Pray to know God—and His church—fully, even as you're known.

But solid food is for the mature, for those whose faculties have been trained by practice to distinguish good from evil.

Hebrews 5:14, NRSV

Some Christian communities feed pablum to members who, presumably, can't swallow the truth unless it's watered down! Most serve whole grains of the gospel or offer meaty, full-course Bible meals. Some try to entice the uncommitted with occasional junk food. A few dish up *just desserts* only!

At the moment, your grandchild needs nothing but milk—no solid food at all. As his or her body begins to develop and mature, your grandson or granddaughter will also require pablum—a milky or watery cereal of cooked rice, oats, barley or rye. Later, when tiny white teeth poke through the little pink gums, your growing grandbaby will have slightly chunkier foods, including fruit, vegetables, and meat.

With the addition of table foods, some parents run small portions of their meals through a food processor. This omits preservatives, cuts costs, and works well when seasonings are omitted. Although a baby could swallow crushed garlic, finely chopped onion, or strong spices, those ingredients would not agree at all with a young child's sensitive, immature system!

In your church and family, immature Christians of every age won't always agree with you! They're not trying to be argumentative or unpleasant, but their delicate systems can't always handle what you need. Nor do you want their pablum or junk food when you require whole grains, meat and veggies!

So, when your grandbaby starts to eat pablum, avoid saying, "Yuck!" As your son or daughter nibbles at what you consider spiritual junk food, be careful not to discourage them from eating at all! Thank God and your family for their desire to feed an immature, but growing, faith in Christ.

Prayer: Dear Heavenly Father, thank You for the variety of spiritual food You bring in Jesus' name.

Journey with God: Are you afraid your child and family aren't well-nourished spiritually? Pray to distinguish your family's needs at various stages of growth. Ask God to help you discern watered-down truth from spiritual food poisoning!

____

____

____

____

____

____

"Look at the birds in the air. They don't plant or harvest or store food in barns, but your heavenly Father feeds them. And you know that you are worth much more than the birds."

Matthew 6:26, NCV

Have you been worried about your family's diet? Are you concerned for their physical, mental, or spiritual nutrition? Do you ever wonder about the quality of their food sources or find yourself thinking things like, "Where on earth did they come up with *that?"* If so, it's time to go bird-watching!

On the shore, sandpipers peck at unseen feasts, eating on the run. Pelicans dive into the sea, loading pouched beaks with fish. Seagulls squeak, like rusty chains on a swing set, as they gleefully glean nutrients from the sandy beach.

In a field, mourning doves coo with delight as seeds drop for their taking. In the forest, red-capped woodpeckers tap the trees and rhythmically uncover hoards of insects. Cardinals flash from limb to limb. Mockingbirds echo. And, on the soft ground, a robin pokes about, looking for fat, ripe worms!

Countless creatures fly and swoop and scurry, seeking food that God provides. Without the tools for planting a harvest, they seek and find what's needed to survive. In fiery days, flood, frost, or famine, the search intensifies. Their desire for food increases, but filled at last, they're satisfied and singing, knowing the goodness that God brings.

So, what do you think? Can this same God be trusted to provide spiritual food for your family? Can He fill your child's hunger to know Him? Can He find a way to draw your grandchild to Himself? Can He uncover your family's need for Him and the nourishment He brings?

Prayer: Heavenly Father, when my child was growing up, it was up to me to provide everything needed. Now that task is no longer mine. It's hard to let go of my old job of meeting my child's now outgrown needs! Forgive me, Lord, for hanging on. I release my family to You and all that You've provided in Jesus' name.

Journey with God: Discuss your fears, feelings, and outgrown responsibilities for childcare. Ask God to help you let go.

Jesus saith unto them, Bring of the fish which ye have now caught.

John 21:10, KJV

As you first begin to let go of the responsibilities you had as a parent, you might feel empty-handed for a while. You might wonder what you'll do with yourself. Or you might fear you've nothing more to tackle. However, as you hand over the job of parenting to your child, you're free to embrace your new job of grandparenting more fully.

Instead of having no tasks or role, you've exchanged one full-time job for another! This new position doesn't center around your grandchild to the exclusion of your daughter or son. You're not the child's parent. You're the parent of a parent—a perfectly grand job to have!

In some ways, your chores have lightened. You're no longer the one who's primarily responsible for the well-being of this new family. You can help if asked, but you don't have to feed, clothe, house, and tend the baby or the child.

Because your child is no longer a child, he or she needs to be treated as an adult. You will allow your daughter or son to make decisions—and mistakes! But you will also enjoy the adult company and mature relationship that's now developing.

To nurture that adult friendship, you may find yourself reverting back to your child's childhood! You might ask your son or daughter to accompany you in activities that the two of you enjoyed years ago. For example, if you used to like fishing, you'll probably enjoy that even more now.

When Jesus' friends went fishing, He asked them to bring Him what they'd caught. To be grand as the parent of a parent, you might do the same! Wait to see what your son or daughter brings to you in friendship, and bring your child some treasure that you've caught yourself.

Prayer: Lord, help me to catch on quickly to this changing time and role! I want to be friends with my child and family in Jesus' name.

Journey with God: Your child needn't be the one who got away! Ask God how you're to reel in your old parenting role with good sportsmanship as you start casting in new waters in your new grandparenting job.

May our sons in their youth be like plants full grown, our daughters like corner pillars, cut for the building of a palace.

Psalm 144:12, NRSV

"Oh, stop acting like a baby! Grow up!" Most parents occasionally want to say that to an adult child—especially if the person acts like an infant when an infant is around! However, as a grandparent, you have a big role in encouraging a new parent's growth.

Right now, for instance, your son or daughter is growing used to the idea of being a dad or mom. No matter what he or she has already encountered, parenting still seems like a loose fit! There are shoes to fill and more growing to do.

Since your child feels—and is—inexperienced, he or she may want to lean on you. That's a comforting, familiar and tempting position for you both! After all, you know how to be a good parent. You have the experience. So, it's easier to take back your old job instead of adjusting to a new one. Unfortunately, this hinders your own growth and your child's.

To encourage your son or daughter to grow up, you'll first have to make that choice too. Gradually, you'll show you're a grand person to count on—not lean on! Demonstrate respect for your son or son-in-law. Allow him to struggle as needed to become a strong Christian, husband, father, son, man, and individual.

Whether or not your daughter or daughter-in-law has another career, applaud her homemaking skills. Show that you just love how she does this or that! Express affection and appreciation for her as a Christian, wife, mother, daughter, woman, and person.

As you watch your child and his or her new family grow, you'll find that you've grown too.

Prayer: Dear holy Father, help me to encourage my family's maturity as I grow up in You in Jesus' name.

Journey with God: In what ways do you feel the Lord wants you to become more mature—socially, emotionally, or spiritually?

____

____

____

____

____

____

____

____

____

____

Day 51

The good leave an inheritance to their children's children.

Proverbs 13:22, NRSV

So, what's the good word? Have you ever thought that your good, affirming words are some of the most valuable inheritances you will ever leave your child? They are!

Sadly, bad words can be handed down too. You've heard them. In crowded schoolrooms, shopping malls, neighborhood streets, playgrounds, and even church school classes, bad words have scraped across your soul like fingernails on a very black board: "Can't you do anything right?" or "Why do you have to be so ugly?" or "You're the stupidest person I've ever seen!" or "I can't stand to be around you!"

Although young children are particularly susceptible, adults often believe what others say about them too. A flat, hard, or pointed statement may have no ring of truth, yet a person might act upon that information as though it's gospel and, eventually, bring it into being.

In these first days when your son or daughter has so little parenting experience, he or she may seem as vulnerable as a small child—and too sensitive to *everything* anyone says! Although you can't give the experience or confidence that's lacking, you're just the person to fill in the missing words: "The baby looks so healthy!" "You're doing such a fine job!"

As you praise what's done well, you give your child and spouse a godly inheritance to pass on to their child. You give healthy, nurturing self-esteem. But most important, you provide the new family with opportunities to trust their growing ability to hear the good word at work in them.

Prayer: Dear Lord, help me to notice, appreciate, and speak of the good I see in my family in Christ's name.

Journey with God: Does your son or daughter lack confidence in some area? Discuss this with God. Ask Him to help you hear His word to speak for the new family's benefit.

A bad messenger brings trouble,
but a faithful envoy, healing.
Proverbs 13:17, NRSV

Remember how years ago your young son or daughter ran to you to tattle? Hopefully, your child outgrew that practice. If not, you may still be caught in the middle of family disputes!

"Mom/Dad, guess what ____ [person's name] did now?"

The answer to that question isn't "Oh, tell me! What?" It's, "No, thanks, dear. I won't guess!" Or, if you prefer, "Uh-uh, I'd rather not hear!"

Encouraging growth means discouraging old, childish ways of coping with family differences. Although tattling may have taken on a more sophisticated adult form, it's still the same game: one person telling on another. Its purpose also remains the same as tattlers try to get someone into trouble so they will appear more angelic themselves!

Bad words stir up trouble. Bad words cast blame. Bad words create sides as family members decide whether they're for or against each other. If the argument or differences occur between your child and his or her spouse, it could bring about their ultimate divorce!

By refusing to take sides or interfere, you take a stand. You grow closer to being a simply grand parent who will be for everyone! You also hold a line that's just right for encouraging prayer. You show love and caring equally to each member of your family.

Prayer: Dear God, when differences arise in my family or bad, harmful words fly, please help me to be a grand peacemaker. I don't want to choose sides, encourage divisions, or get caught between squabbles! Help me to take an impartial stand on behalf of each person in my family. Help me to show love equally and to give equal prayer time for every member of my family in Christ's name.

Journey with God: Ask God how you're to make clear that the only side you're on is His!

But the wisdom from above is first pure, then peaceable, gentle, willing to yield, full of mercy and good fruits, without a trace of partiality or hypocrisy.

James 3:17, NRSV

Do you have any gray hair yet? For some reason, people think the whiter the hair, the wiser the person, and that's about half right! Wisdom does comes from above hair level!

Although you probably won't ever pray to be gray, you will want the wisdom that comes from above. James 1:5 says, "If any of you is lacking in wisdom, ask God, who gives to all generously and ungrudgingly, and it will be given you" (NRSV).

Whether people ask for it or not, white hair eventually comes to everyone who lives long enough! To those who ask for wisdom, God gives generously to all. He shows no partiality or favoritism to anyone in His family.

Have you done the same? Have you impartially given good and wise gifts to each family member? Or have you at times favored one person over another?

Most people do have someone in their family with whom they connect—someone with whom they can easily share values, goals, beliefs, feelings, tastes, or humor. If this has happened in your experience, naturally you enjoy that person's company. You're more relaxed and more yourself.

That's fine! However, problems come when a parent shows favoritism by giving in to a child's whims or by giving more attention and affection to one child than to another. So, get wise! Get God's wisdom, and put it to work—generously and impartially—in your family.

Prayer: Dear Lord, forgive me for the times I have played favorites. Please help my family to forgive me too! I need Your wisdom and Your love for everyone You bring into my family and my life in Jesus' name.

Journey with God: Talk with God about the ways you've shown partiality. Be specific as you make notes in this space. Use the notes as reminders to pray for each family member.

___

___

___

___

___

___

___

___

___

___

___

But the wisdom that comes from God is like this: first, it is pure. Then it is also peaceful, gentle, and easy to please. This wisdom is always ready to help those who are troubled and to do good for others. This wisdom is always fair and honest.

James 3:17, NCV

Would your family say you're easy to please? Would they say that ALL of the time? Probably not! No one can easily be pleased every minute of every day. So, when you're displeased about something—anything—get rid of the accompanying bad attitude *before* you try to do good! Don't step forward to help your family until you've backed up a bit.

From the start, God's wisdom comes in the purest form of love. So every motive for every word and action first needs to line up with that pureness. When you're satisfied you have no impure motives in giving this or doing that for someone, *then* you take the next step toward making peace.

You already know, of course, that whatever you do or say to make peace in your family starts with a peaceable attitude or spirit within yourself. This, too, comes as a result of pureness in your relationship with God.

Do you see a wise pattern here? According to God's Word, you'll be purely fair, purely honest, purely helpful, purely gentle, purely peaceable, and, yes, purely easy to please, as you rely on pure wisdom—God's, not yours! But remember: God said His wisdom *is* yours if you want it!

Who could ask for anything more? What finer gift could you give your child, grandchild, or another family member than the wisdom God Himself has given you? From the start of your grandparenting days, He will give you the wisdom to pour His pure love into your family!

Prayer: Holy Father, I praise You for Your pure love and pure wisdom! Thank You for giving this to me to give to my family in Jesus' name.

Journey with God: Is there some area of your life where you feel you need to "wise up" more? Discuss this with God. Let His wisdom cover you.

___

___

___

___

___

___

___

___

___

___

___

Day 55

For by grace are ye saved through faith; and that not of yourselves: it is the gift of God: Not of works, lest any man should boast.

Ephesians 2:8–9, KJV

Is your child hard to please? Does insistence on his or her way create problems for other people? Do you feel even more concerned now that your child has a family? Does this cause you personal stress or distress?

If your son or daughter has said, "Mom/Dad, *you're* the problem," that could be true! If so, talk with God about the specific situation, character trait or tendency, and confess any wrongdoing. Ask God to help you overcome that flaw, but also ask Him to help you refuse any *false* guilts!

Like most parents, you did the best you could. Even if you tried very hard to be Supermom or Superdad, you did not succeed! No one does. The important thing now is to help your son or daughter realize this fact too.

Perhaps your child won't be ready to admit similar flaws or personal failures. That's up to every individual and to God. Meanwhile, you can show your faith in your child and his or her ability to be a good parent. Tell the new mom or dad, "I'm proud of you!" Continue to pray for the family. But you won't make things right by encouraging people to expect perfection in you, themselves, or anyone else!

Only God is perfect. The sooner your child knows this, the better! Although you can't force your son or daughter to understand, you can make yourself face that truth. You can choose to have faith, not in what your child says about you, but what God's Word says about you! He says you are saved from the penalty of mistakes and imperfection by His forgiving grace.

Prayer: Heavenly Father, forgive me for expecting my child or myself to be perfect—and, worse, for pretending that it's true! Thank You for Your gift of forgiveness, made perfect only in Christ Jesus. Help me to have the grace to forgive myself and others always in Christ's name.

Journey with God: Talk with God about areas in your family that need perfecting through acceptance and confession of real guilt and refusal of false guilt.

____

____

____

____

____

____

____

____

If you have ears, then, listen to what the Spirit says to the churches!

Revelation 2:7, TEV (repeated in 2:11, 17, 29, and 3:6, 13, 22)

Graciously accepting criticism from your family is one thing. Graciously giving it is another! You need to prepare yourself for both!

For example, if you see your child and his or her spouse developing poor parenting skills, you'll need to address that issue, prayerfully with God and privately with them. Your son or daughter may be consistently losing sleep, eating poorly, or trying so hard to be perfect that he or she can't seem to do anything right!

A word of empathy, love and encouragement may be all that's needed. However, if your child has begun to take out a bad mood on the baby, you'll need to speak immediately and directly to this situation. Before you say anything, though, listen to what the Holy Spirit says to you!

Chapters 2 and 3 of the Book of Revelation reveals Jesus' pattern of speaking to His family, the church. Here's His godly example that you can wisely follow:

(1) The Lord first found something encouraging to say. He began His private word to each church by speaking of the things they do well—if in fact, anything is!

(2) The Lord went straight to the point—and the heart of a problem. He described what's wrong in a brief,

direct manner.

(3) The Lord clearly spelled out the consequences should the sin or wrongdoing continue.

(4) The Lord ended each discussion with a specific promise and His encouraging word. He personally guaranteed the good that will come to those who hear and heed His will.

Prayer: Dear Lord, help me to be ready to obey by quickly listening to what You have to say to me in Jesus' holy name.

Journey with God: If you're unsure whether to speak or keep silent about your child's behavior, ask yourself: Is it up to me to say something? If so, what? Better yet, ask God!

Those who love me, I will deliver; I will protect those who know my name. When they call to me, I will answer them; I will be with them in trouble, I will rescue them and honor them.

Psalm 91:14–15, NRSV

"Am I a fit parent or not?" Most parents ask themselves that, especially in the beginning of their parenting days. Your son or daughter probably wonders too, so naturally, you will do what you can to provide reassurance. But what about your own questions? Do you now wonder if you're fit to be a grandparent? If so, let God's Word reassure you!

Being a fit grandparent means you're mentally competent and well equipped for the job. Since God Himself has given you the benefits of His guidance, power, and protection, you aren't just well equipped! You're wonderfully equipped!

Can you say the same about your mental faculties? Well, that depends on how well balanced you are! For example, if something awful happens, does your mind weigh that heavy set of circumstances against the mental leverage of knowing God is in charge? Do you trust Him to be with you and bring good?

You will if you love Him! How can you help but love Someone who stands by you, takes care of you, and always loves you?

If you're not 100 percent sure how well God's love fits you personally, get to know Him intimately. As you read

His Word from cover to cover, you'll uncover the truth about Him. You'll see Him as He is, was, and will be forever. The more you learn *about* Him, the more you'll want to know Him well. Isn't that fitting? To know God *is* to love Him!

Prayer: Dear God, I thought I knew You, but I guess I just know what I've always heard, thought, or assumed. Help me to recognize You as You are in the full light of Jesus' name.

Journey with God: To know and love God more: (1) Ask Him to fit the *whole* Bible into *your realistic reading* schedule! (It takes no longer than reading a lengthy novel! Most people can do that several times a year; some several times a month!) (2) Using a Bible concordance, look up names or attributes of God's character. Meditate on several favorites in the space below.

___

___

___

___

___

___

___

___

But for you who revere my name the sun of righteousness shall rise, with healing in its wings. You shall go out leaping like calves from the stall.

Malachi 4:2, NRSV

If you've been physically helping your son or daughter, you've remembered how taxing child care can be! Bending over a crib, shouldering a diaper bag, lugging laundry, or carrying the baby, you've discovered muscles you'd forgotten you had!

To stay physically fit for grandparenting, what you need to do is this: *Take care of yourself as well as you would your grandchild!* Consider your minimum daily requirements for food, sleep, and exercise. Then find a healthy balance by prayerfully and realistically evaluating those areas.

For instance, many people seem to think they'll be healthier if they omit *all* sugar, salt, and fat from their diet, but that probably isn't healthy for anyone! For some, it can be dangerous to do completely without or to substitute artificial ingredients for what a body just naturally needs!

Find out what works best for you. Investigate. Talk to a doctor about your physical tendencies. Read up on nutrition. Don't be concerned about what's faddish or what other people need! Be realistic about the meals and snacks *you* need!

The same applies to rest and exercise. Just because most people need eight hours of sleep doesn't mean you do! Maybe that much would make you groggy. Or maybe you need nine hours to feel refreshed. And, just because everyone you know pumps iron doesn't mean you need bodybuilding. Daily exercise that flexes your joints and muscles or increases circulation could be healthier. You might just need a half hour walk to flex your faith as you energetically leap into prayer!

Prayer: Dear Lord, You know every ache and pain I have! Help me to exercise in the fresh air of Your Holy Spirit and the healing Sonshine of Jesus' name.

Journey with God: Have you been taking good care of everyone but yourself? Repent! Seek God's personal word for your physical fitness. Ask Him how you're to shape up!

Because thou hast made the LORD, which is my refuge, even the most High, thy habitation; There shall no evil befall thee, neither shall any plague come nigh thy dwelling. For he shall give his angels charge over thee, to keep thee in all thy ways.

Psalm 91:9–11, KJV

Are you spiritually fit for grandparenting? You don't have to wonder about your spiritual shape and condition or whether you've religiously "arrived." In Christ, you can be certain. In Him, you can be fully at home with God.

Jesus called Himself "the door," "the gate" and "the way" because, in spiritual reality, that's exactly what He is! He provides the only spiritual access for you to come to your Heavenly Father. His holiness provides wholeness which snugly fits you into God's family—and God's Spirit into you!

You'll be assured of spiritual fitness as you act on this reality. To help you better see, picture yourself in an enclosure that cannot be penetrated by even the strongest forces. Right outside the door awaits every kind of evil. Infernal plagues camp out. Heavy-duty weaponry aims at your soul. Massive artillery points toward your spirit.

As you can imagine, there's nothing on earth you can do to save yourself from such a vast and evil army. But, praise God, you don't have to defend yourself! Christ Himself has got you covered! He shields you with His own body and blood.

For those who have not yet hid themselves in Christ, very real spiritual dangers do exist. Violence, disaster, ill will, and ill health haven't yet retreated for all time. But, as you stay inside God's will, nothing that befalls can bring you down. No evil power on earth or in heaven can annihilate the love of God which is in Christ Jesus.

Prayer: Praise You, Father, for keeping me in Your protective custody in Christ's name!

Journey with God: In what ways do you try to defend yourself or your own position? Talk with God about the spiritual territory He's set for you within the unlimited boundaries of Christ's love.

Bring me out of prison, so that I may give thanks to your name. The righteous will surround me, for you will deal bountifully with me.

Psalm 142:7, NRSV

Has your son or daughter gotten into a bind? Does the new family seem to be walled in by heavy debt, hard feelings, rigid demands, or set-in-cement expectations? Are they *bound* to repeat their mistakes or be sentenced to the consequences?

Imprisonment comes in many forms, but most types confine the body, mind, or spirit to cramped quarters where there's little room for movement and growth. In especially close-knit families, other people may feel like inmates too. A spouse, child, or parent can be held as an emotional hostage to fear, embarrassment, or ongoing disruptions in the family's life.

If you suspect your son or daughter has become captive to something or has been detained by dependency, don't expect a quick fix. Everything *won't* be OK as soon as you think of *the* right word or do *the* right thing!

Your child's deliverance does not depend on you. Nor can you help by being a prop or by enabling bad habits. For example, if you rush in with cash or another temporary form of bail whenever a problem arises, you will only delay your child's final release from bondage.

You also need to know it's very hard being outside the situation, yet not free to help. Imprisonment greatly affects those who come to visit. But, thanks to the saving power of Jesus Christ, you're God's own righteous child! Your love and prayers keep your child and family surrounded no matter how long freedom, independence or salvation takes! Despite the depth of prison walls, God's love will penetrate. The name of Jesus will prevail.

Prayer: Heavenly Father, I praise You for Your ability to save all peoples in all situations! Thank You for not confining Your love to those who deserve it. Thank You for sending Your healing help to all who ask in Jesus' name.

Journey with God: What walls exist in your family? Ask God to surround you with His prayers to pray for each family member who's incarcerated in some way. Thank Him for releasing you!

____

____

____

____

____

____

____

Let my cry come before you, O LORD; give me understanding according to your word. Let my supplication come before you; deliver me according to your promise.

Psalm 119:169–70, NRSV

Did you hear about Monica? She had the most wayward, impossible son! Long after he'd grown up, he kept acting like a child, but Monica just would not give up on him. For years, she prayed for her son's release from captivating evils. She sought God with such unwavering faith, people said, "What a saint!" When her child finally did repent, the change was so dramatic that some called him a saint too—Saint Augustine.

In the Bible, the apostle Paul referred to the saints who suffered deprivation and physical threats or torture because of faith in Christ. Today, Christian parents and grandparents often face torment within their own families because their standards clash with the world's. This also calls for saintly faith—not in yourself or your child, but in God's Word.

When Monica prayed for her son's deliverance, she agreed with God's will—applicable to *every* son and daughter! When you pray in His will, you're in agreement with what God wants anyway! It's not that He *can't* work without prayers, but the Good Parent prefers to help *after* being asked, not before!

As you ponder God's Word, you become more aware of His will for your family. You see His promises and any conditions He may have attached—conditions that need to be fulfilled. Once they are, you can claim those Bible promises in prayer as though God is just this very moment speaking to you and your family. Actually, He is!

Prayer: Dear Lord, I don't always understand what the Bible says, but I trust You to reveal Your meaning and promises to me before I need to know! Thank You for sending Your Holy Spirit to guide my reading of Your Word in Jesus' name.

Journey with God: Look for Bible promises that apply to your concerns. Discuss any conditions with God. Then list specific promises you can rightfully claim on your family's behalf.

___

___

___

___

___

___

___

___

___

Day 62

Children are a gift from the LORD;
they are a real blessing.

Psalm 127:3, TEV

Reading God's Word, you'll find more than Bible promises to claim for your family. From "In the beginning" to the last "Amen," God's truths come to you for the claiming too!

For example, today's verse says that children are a gift and a blessing from God. So your response won't be, "Yeah, right!" or, "Who says?" God says! In His Word on children, God declares them a gift and a blessing. Therefore, you can respond, "Well, I declare!"

At the moment you might feel just the opposite of that declaration—especially if your child has become entrapped in a troublesome situation or seems headed for destruction. Maybe the new family hasn't adjusted well, and divorce seems inevitable. Or, perhaps your grandchild's health has begun to deteriorate, and you're just plain scared. No one can promise that your descendants will flourish or even survive. No one can say if your grandchild will be gifted or handicapped. No one knows if your son or daughter will bless you by choosing godly standards for their families or if they'll consistently make poor choices. But everyone who knows and believes God knows this: *Your* children are a gift from God. (Say their names now.) *Your* children are a blessing.

The more that seems to mock you, the more you need to face this truth in prayer. God does not lie. He always means what He says, so *choose* to place your faith in Him. Make up your mind to believe what He says more than you believe the conditions or ill words around you. If God's Word isn't true for you right now, claim His truth for your family. Declare!

Prayer: Dear Lord, thank You for the blessing of letting me know that my child and grandchild are a gift from You. I declare the truth of Your Word for my family in Jesus' name.

Journey with God: As you read the Bible at home or hear God's Word in a church service, note Scriptures that speak to you personally. Claim those as you journal.

____

____

____

____

____

____

____

____

"People cry out for help when they are in trouble. They beg for relief from powerful people. But no one asks, 'Where is God, my Maker? He gives us songs in the night.'"

Job 35:9–10, NCV

"Why, God? Why me?"

When nothing seems to be going well, people want to know *why*. That's only natural. Asking, "Why do you suppose this happened?" can help people pinpoint a precise problem and then consider workable solutions.

It's also only natural to cry out, "Help!" to God in times of trouble. People who might not turn to Him otherwise may be drawn close to Him during trying times. As they realize how powerless they are to help a wounded or hostile child or an ill grandchild, they might seek the One who has all power.

But, sometimes people go beyond what's only natural. Sometimes they enter what's only supernatural by demanding God to give them an accounting of Himself or His actions. "Why, God?" they ask, but God owes them no explanation! He cannot take credit for the presence of sin in the world nor a lack of faithful prayer within the Christian community!

God provides good. Even in awful circumstances, He wants to be trusted. He wants you to ask, "God, where are You in this situation?" Then He can reassure you, "I am here."

At times, you cannot help but wonder what God is doing or perhaps, if you're to blame. It's only natural that you'd want to know. And, as a Christian, naturally you'll want to correct what you can. You might pray for forgiveness, mercy, strength, relief or protection. But, in the darkest hour of affliction, you can listen for God's *comfort* to *come for* you! Listen as God your Maker brings you His song in the night.

Prayer: Almighty God, help me to hear Your hope and feel Your strength in the saving song of Jesus' name.

Journey with God: Attune yourself to hearing God's refrain of love that comes to you through the pages of the Bible and in the life, death, and resurrection of Jesus Christ. List lyrics of Scripture that particularly speak to you. Let them sing!

____

____

____

____

____

____

____

____

Your statutes have been my songs wherever I make my home.

Psalm 119:54, NRSV

"Hey! That's just how it is! If you're going to live under *my* roof, you'd better get used to it!" Do you need to sing that tune? Maybe so! If your son or daughter had to move back home to provide a place for the baby, you probably established some rules to keep everything running smoothly.

Basic rules cover basic needs, not only for the baby, but everyone in the house. If one person wants something that conflicts with what another really needs, adjustments have to be made. Family members can learn to consider each other's requirements for nourishment, sleep, work, play, and privacy.

As you work out household rules and privileges, you'll note that some schedules and needs remain constant; others do not. In many situations, you can try to be flexible, yet you may have to orchestrate firm guidelines in the very areas where the most flexibility exists!

For example, the Bible doesn't say, "Thou shalt not awaken your parents by coming in late." Nor does it caution your child against canceling your dinner plans by emptying the refrigerator during the day! However, God's Word does encourage children of all ages to respect a parent's needs and to sing along with a parent's requests!

The more you know God's Word, the more you'll hum through each new situation that arises. Meanwhile, if you're unsure how to sing, the Golden Rule provides a consistently steady rhythm for your family. By treating others in the house as *you want* to be treated, relationships won't get off key! They'll be harmonious as you stay in tune with God's Word—and as you play by the ear that He's given to you.

Prayer: Dear God, having an adult child at home means a lot of sacrifices I hadn't expected! I'm not thrilled to give up my privacy or preferences even when the new family comes to visit, much less stay! In Jesus' name, help me always follow Your lead for my household.

Journey with God: What adjustments need to be made to keep everyone harmonizing at your home with God's will?

____

____

____

____

____

____

____

"Then I will lead the blind along a way they never knew; I will guide them along paths they have not known. I will make the darkness become light for them. And I will make the rough ground smooth. These are the things I will do. I will not leave my people."

Isaiah 42:16, NCV

Does your son or daughter live in another town? Do you go see your grandchild occasionally instead of always hosting visits? If the new parents feel good about their home and themselves, they'll probably be glad for your company!

Besides the advantage of seeing new sights and scenes, travel gives you the opportunity to think and pray. Naturally you'll be thinking about the family you're going to visit, so ask God to bring His thoughts to light in your prayers.

You might also pass the time listening to your favorite songs, hymns or religious programs on a radio or tape player. If you go by train or plane, you'll probably need a headset, and in the car, you'll just turn up the speakers to hear the music or the news. Either way, you'll find a travel companion in God's Word. Instead of listening to a radio newscast, pop in a tape and listen to the good news!

People who aren't fond of reading welcome the Bible on tape. Yet, if you're the proverbial bookworm, Proverbs and other books of the Bible will come alive as you *hear* them spoken into being. That's how they were originally meant to be read—aloud! So, as you listen you'll hear the poetic cadence which soothes a travel-worn body, mind, and spirit.

God's Word has impact and power. His stories guide. His truths lead you straight ahead. If you haven't traveled this way before, you might hear a phrase or message you'd never noticed. As you go great distances with God, you'll be more aware that He's beside you. You'll have His Word on it!

Prayer: Dear Father, help me to be at home in Your will and Your Word wherever I go in Christ's name.

Journey with God: As you travel, journey with God along the route of His Word. Keep a travelogue of what you hear.

____

____

____

____

____

____

____

____

____

*"When you pass through the waters,
I will be with you. When you cross
rivers, you will not drown.
When you walk through fire,
you will not be burned.
The flames will not hurt you."*

Isaiah 43:2, NCV

"Over the river and through the woods, to Grandmother's house we go!" Traditionally, family members have sung that song as holidays bring them together in the grandparents' home. If you like those lyrics, sing! But, if you live in a condo, manufactured home park, or retirement complex, you might want to change the tune!

Maybe you don't like to bake holiday cookies! Maybe you wish your family or a local restaurant would cater to you!

Maybe you're tired of planning festivities or decorating the house or cleaning up the mess. Maybe you're just tired! Since your son or daughter can't read your mind, you'll need to tell them what you think. Start by letting them know how very much you want to see them and your grandchild during the holidays. Don't assume they already know! Be clear. Then announce, "Let's do something different this year."

Offer options, and give each person a say in how they'd like to spend their holidays too. If someone volunteers, "I really would like to host a family get-together," why not let them? If someone says, "We don't have room at our house, but I'd be glad to cook dinner," don't say no. Say, "Thanks!"

If someone suggests, "We could each bring a covered dish, and eat in the park," do it!

As you make new plans, be aware that some family members won't like the idea of any changes. Some might be so miffed, they'll stay at home. But, as you ask God to plan and protect your holidays, emotional fires needn't burn you. Hurt tempers won't flare forever. And you won't drown in a deluge of work!

Prayer: Dear Lord, please help my family cross over times of change without crossing each other! Help us to be thoughtful of one another and place our expectations only in You in Jesus' name.

Journey with God: What do you expect from your family during the holidays? Ask God how you can communicate your thoughts and feelings clearly and lovingly.

"Bring my sons from far away and my daughters from faraway places. Bring to me all the people who are mine, whom I made for my glory, whom I formed and made."

Isaiah 43:6–7, NCV

During Christmas, Easter or other holy day celebrations, most grandparents enjoy buying or making gifts. If you have close contact with your family throughout the year, you'll have a pretty good idea of what would be appropriate or appreciated. If not, ask!

During special occasions, people often get caught up in elaborate preparations intended to surprise each other. That can be a lot of fun unless the big surprise comes when no one likes what they've received! Feelings get hurt, and holidays turn into memorably bad occasions!

In this first year of your grandbaby's life, your son or daughter and spouse will know what's needed. Later, when your grandchild is old enough to have preferences, naturally, you will ask, "What would you like for me to get you this year?" However, the parents will continue to appreciate your asking them about unusual or costly gifts, especially if a present would affect their own values or beliefs.

For instance, parents who abhor violence will not be too thrilled to have someone give their child a war toy! Most parents will not welcome massive doses of candy or anything they deem unhealthy for their child. Dishonoring such opinions could influence a child to dishonor his or her parents.

As you prepare for holiday gift giving, talk with your family and God. Ask what good gifts He wants you to give for His name's sake. Thank Him for bringing your family together and making each of you a gift—one He bought for Himself and shares with you all!

Prayer: Heavenly Father, I praise You for the gift of Your Son in whose name I pray that my family comes together during this season and on each holy day of the year.

Journey with God: On this special journaling occasion, bring to God the gift of your family and yourself. Give Him praise and appreciation for all He's done for you.

But the LORD *says, "Do not cling to events of the past or dwell on what happened long ago. Watch for the new thing I am going to do. It is happening already— you can see it now!"*

Isaiah 43:18–19, TEV

Do family get-togethers ever become a hassle? Does each person seem to expect your full favor, time, and attention? If you have two or more children, do old habits, rivalries, or jealousies ignite in each other's company? Now that one child has a child, have feelings and emotions become heated?

According to God's Word, it doesn't have to be that way! Regardless of family size or placement, each person has *some* cause for complaint! Nobody's perfect. Mistakes are made. And sometimes people just get on each other's nerves! But you don't have to expect or even accept such heated conditions.

It may take a while for your children to let go of their past hurts or disappointments. It could take years for them to stop feeling like a little kid every time they're together—especially when they're in your home! However, you can do your part in claiming God's Word for your family by seeing your children as adults—by not living in the past.

If emotions have already flared, you might have to tell each person to leave home any childhood fires that still burn others in the family! You can also offer to pray with someone who feels anxious, angry, or wounded, continuing of course to uplift each family member in your private prayers.

If you must discuss old problems, be honest, forgiving, and lovingly direct. Ask God to turn upsetting memories into clear reminders of His presence. Let Him bless your gathering in His name. Then watch out! Look for new relationships and good things to come to your family—now!

Prayer: Dear Lord, help my family to enjoy Your present company in Christ's name.

Journey with God: What has your family been clinging to that has hindered your relationships with each other and with God? What solutions has He helped you now see?

____

____

____

____

____

____

____

____

____

"Do not be afraid—I am with you! From the distant east and the farthest west I will bring your people home."

Isaiah 43:5, TEV

Do members of your family have to travel a long distance to get together? That's possible even if they live just down the street!

Since the beginning of time, children have challenged their parents' customs, beliefs, values, and traditions. Most reject something their parents say, at least for a while. Perhaps they marry someone from another culture—one that seems foreign by opposing all their parents hold dear.

When everyone comes together for a special occasion, the diverse backgrounds can make a family interesting or at odds. Often such differences become delightful as a family expands to include an assortment of colorful customs and traditions. However, differences and distances can seem to increase when someone says a blessing over the meal!

If your child and spouse have "headed west" into Western humanism or "gone east" to Eastern religions, you'll need to pronounce God's grace! Before anyone arrives, claim His peace and healing word for this special occasion.

Rely on God's Word that promises to draw all peoples to Himself. Request His presence and power. Claim whatever is called for as you call for God's help! And if you're the one giving a blessing for a meal, don't be shy! Declare the name of Jesus over the food and your family.

Prayer: Heavenly Father, I know You don't want dissension among Your children, so You understand when I say I don't either! Give me Your wisdom to speak with truth and Your love to bear the differences among us. Help me to say grace with grace—and ongoing faith in Your Name.

Journey with God: Are you afraid of the conflicts or tensions that could arise as some Western philosophy or Eastern religion threatens to ruin a family get-together? Give God your fears! Ask Him what and when you're to speak. Ask how you're to rely on Him and His timing in bringing your family home to Him.

Day 70

All this is from God, who reconciled us to himself through Christ, and has given us the ministry of reconciliation.

2 Corinthians 5:18, NRSV

Did your child used to play follow the leader? When you were small, perhaps you did too. The game has similarities to being the grand marshal of a parade—or the grandparent of a family gathering!

As you set a pace or mood for others during a holiday get-together, start on the right foot by following Christ's lead. Ask His Holy Spirit to help you lay down self-centered desires and personal preferences. Place them on the cross—the point at which your will runs counter to God's.

In His supreme, holy, complete sacrifice on His cross, Jesus Christ reconciled you to God. He made up the difference between you and the Heavenly Father. Now He—not you—can make up the difference between members of your family.

With the help of His Holy Spirit, Christ brings prayer needs to your attention. You'll become aware of moody faces, miffed feelings, or rising voices—not to involve you in disputes, but to pray for God's love and peace to prevail.

As you become sensitive to the Lord's leading, you'll perceive genuine needs. The Holy Spirit will let you know. This embrace of empathy, affection, appreciation, or attention may be all that's needed to reconcile one person to another. Everyone wants to be wanted! With Christ's Spirit to lead you, you'll show welcome as you encircle each family member with a word of thanksgiving and love. Sometimes that won't be easy—especially if someone has crossed you! But beyond the cross comes reconciliation—with yourself, other people, and God.

Prayer: Dear Father, thank You for giving me a ministry of reconciliation to my family. Help me to remember that this gift comes not from myself, but from You in Jesus' name.

Journey with God: Does your family harbor any irreconcilable differences? Offer these to God in prayer. Seek His insight and private word to you about each situation.

So then, putting away falsehood, let all of us speak the truth to our neighbors, for we are members of one another.

Ephesians 4:25, NRSV

"Don't you lie to me!" Did you ever say that to your child? Why? What gave you the first clue?

Shuffling feet and slouching posture, or the opposite—a jutted chin and defiant stance—sometimes provide telltale signs that a person is telling a tale but not the truth! But as an adult, your son or daughter could be so clever at disguises, he or she doesn't realize any falsehoods exist!

When things go badly, some adults lie to themselves. They totally blame others, such as a spouse or sibling, for their problems. They especially blame parents! But they can also put on so many layers of guilt or self-condemnation they can't face a mirror, much less a family gathering!

For a temporary problem, such as the fatigue new parents suffer from lack of sleep, your empathy could be all that's necessary to help them see the truth: "You just need some rest!" But, if your child consistently argues, withdraws, rebels, or has chronically poor perception, he or she may be holding onto a faulty view of self or family.

Besides keeping that person in your private prayers, you might ask, "Is everything OK?" Opening a conversation can help strip away layers of falsehood. Frank discussions also give you the opportunity to say, "Would it be OK with you if we pray about this now?"

Your child or other family members might not be ready to pray—or even talk! But they'll know that you're available and you care. On this memorable occasion, the special people in your life will see that the truth doesn't scare you! So when they're ready to face it, they'll know they can trust you to be prayerfully and lovingly honest with them.

Prayer: Oh, God! Help me to put away all falsehoods—about myself, my family, and You—in Jesus' name.

Journey with God: As a family faces the truth, they come back together. Each *member* begins to *re-member* the others! Ask God to help you remember what needs healing or reconciling to Him.

Now this I affirm and insist on in the Lord: you must no longer live as the Gentiles live, in the futility of their minds. They are darkened in their understanding, alienated from the life of God because of their ignorance and hardness of heart.

Ephesians 4:17–18, NRSV

"Hey! I mean business! Stop kidding around! No more games!" Have you ever insisted that family members quit evading issues and face the truth? If so, you've realized that old responses to one another need to change!

As people grow, relationships also grow—closer or farther apart. However, spurts of growth vary from one person to another, so everyone won't be ready to grow a relationship at the same time. If something unfortunate occurs (as it does in every family on occasion) that setback could temporarily halt development.

Eventually, healthy persons will try to readapt, reheal, and renew growth. But, some people still might not renew relationships they see as harmful! Some may need more time for tentative self-growth before they become entangled with family members. Some won't know how to get any closer to a parent, sibling, or spouse. Some will be too timid to try.

God understands. He knows that fears, ignorance, hurts, and hardness of heart can separate people. He also knows that such attitudes not only separate families—including church families—but they distance individuals from Him.

Even though God understands what's happening, His Word says stop! He wants His children to stop futile thinking, childish games, and dark thoughts that alienate them from each other. He wants them to stop acting like people who have no faith, no hope, no God! He wants you to forgive yourself and one another in the Lord.

Prayer: God, help my family to accept our rightful place in Your family in Jesus' name.

Journey with God: Is anyone in your family ignorant about God? Does anyone seem locked into dark and hopeless thoughts or act as though they think faith in God is futile? Consider what alienates that person from the Lord. Ask for His light to show you how to pray for them.

"They are the people I made for myself, and they will sing my praises!"

Isaiah 43:21, TEV

Before family get-togethers, do you first get together every photograph you have to show of your grandchild? Naturally you want to sing the baby's praises! After all, this is undoubtedly the most gorgeous, intelligent, well-coordinated, good-humored, winsome child God ever created—right?

You do want the truth, don't you? Well, the truth is, *every* child of God is the most wonderful, most precious child to Him! Unlike you, He has no grandchildren! So, He's proud of each person He created in His image. Son or daughter, He calls to each one, "Very good!"

After sin darkened His children's faces, God sent His Son to bring back the light. Since His holiness could not accept their evil deeds or hateful acts, He gave His light to Jesus and asked Him to bring His children back into His full view. Christ did. In Him, God's children are fully illuminated in His light.

As your family gets together, look for that light. Take lots of photographs of your grandchild and of other people—expressions and scenes that reveal their love as they talk, play, and enjoy one another. Make the most of the occasion!

God made the most of you! He brought you together, and He deserves the praise. So, thank Him for your family. Praise His holy name. Give Him credit for every good thing you see or picture in each person. Pray they each become all that God made them to be.

Prayer: Heavenly Father, sometimes I've wanted so much for my child to look or act a certain way that I haven't always seen the full picture You had in mind. Forgive me, Lord. Help me to trust You to bring my child and each member of this family into the fullness of all You made them to be in Jesus' name.

Journey with God: Have you felt displeased when your child or another family member suddenly moved from the direction you had in mind? Show God your marred picture. Then swap photos with Him! Ask for His view of what He intends this person to be.

Day 74

The Lord *said to me, "I chose you before I gave you life, and before you were born I selected you to be a prophet to the nations."*

Jeremiah 1:4, TEV

At family gatherings, adults often ask children, "What do you want to be when you grow up?" Typically, preschoolers respond that they want to fight fires, germs, or bad guys. Some want to take people places in taxis, trains, planes, ambulances, or race cars!

By school age, children frequently want to be teachers, preachers, or other types of professionals who impart truths, wisdom, or information. Some want to express themselves creatively, through art, literature, music, or new inventions. Some plan to travel the world or set world records.

Long before your grandchild considers a career choice, you'll also start to speculate: *What will this child become?* As you examine his or her tiny fingers, you may already wonder if those hands will skillfully play a piano or initiate a delicate sequence on a computer! Will that little nose sniff out news or that little mouth detect the separate ingredients in a secret recipe?

Almost from the start, you'll see familiar family traits developing. You'll note mental alertness, physical strength, and signs of personality, and you'll wonder how they'll fit together as this child grows up. But, as a Christian, you'll also wonder, *What will my grandchild become in Christ?*

In some ways, that's up to you and your son or daughter! Your family can provide the needed environment, education, and encouragement. You can surround this child with love and prayer. Yet everything won't be your responsibility! Each uniquely tailored experience and ability will come from God's purpose, depending on what *He intends* this child to be.

Prayer: Heavenly Father, thank You for having something valuable and worthy in mind for my grandchild. Help us to know Your special plans for each of us in Jesus' name.

Journey with God: Do you feel chosen by God for a particular task? Does your son or daughter? Ask God how He wants you to encourage the use of His good gifts for His good purpose in your family.

____

____

____

____

____

____

____

"I am the LORD who created you;
from the time you were born I have
helped you. Do not be afraid;
you are my servant,
my chosen people whom I love."

Isaiah 44:2, TEV

"I'm always hearing about the baby! Can't we talk about something else for a while?" If you have another child at home or nearby, he or she may be tired of conversations about your grandchild. Your husband or wife might feel the same. Or maybe you wish the new parents would sometimes ask how *you're* doing instead of always telling you what the baby does!

In the first few months of parenting, the new mother and father sharply focus their attention on their baby, often to the exclusion of other interests. That's only natural as the family adjusts to one another. Naturally, as the new grandfather or grandmother, you want to tell everyone all about this wonderful first addition. However, a first edition book or first run movie might rate more interest from other household members, and that's only natural too!

During times of change or adjustment, each person in your family fears that nothing will ever be the same. Another son or daughter may even be afraid you love the new parent and child so much, no one else matters! Your spouse might feel left out, or perhaps you do when the new family visits, time and again, with only one topic of conversation—the baby!

Whether they ask or not, you and everyone else in your family wants to know, "Do you still love me? Are you still glad I'm around? Do you still choose my company?"

God does! Time after time, people focus on their own lives to the exclusion of their Lord and Maker. Then they act as though He's wandered away from them! He hasn't. God stays near. He still desires the presence of your company. He still loves you and wants you to get together with Him—forever!

Prayer: Heavenly Father, help me to be still and hear Your topic of conversation for me this day in Jesus' name.

Journey with God: Who in your family has tired of baby talk? Talk with God about ways you can reassure each person of your love—and His!

Day 76

Let the words of my mouth,
and the meditation of my heart,
be acceptable in thy sight, O LORD,
my strength, and my redeemer.

Psalm 19:14, KJV

"So, what do you want to talk about?"

"I don't know. What do you want to talk about?"

"Something!"

When new parents or grandparents become eager to talk about almost anything, that's a sign they've been cooped up too long! At first, it's only natural to think of nothing but the baby, yet a family eventually needs to expand interests!

Similar feelings occur during any time of change or crisis. Typically, a family focuses on one person or problem to the exclusion of almost everything else. That's healthy when love and support surround the people involved or when everyone's attention brings about possible solutions to the problem. But heavy duty concentration on one individual or situation makes it difficult to think about other matters.

Eventually, the same old thoughts get boring! That's nothing to be ashamed of; it indicates it's time for other topics, time to expand interests, relationships, and something besides one's waist or worries! It's time to consider, "What's new?"

As you and other people adjust to the changes in your families, you'll be ready to think again! The new baby will continue to need loving attention, but adults in the family will need to resume their activities and goals too.

Before thinking about something new—much less talking about it—let God speak to your heart. Listen to His plans for you, and encourage your child to do the same. Seek His strength of mind to focus your attention where it belongs—on Him. Meditate on His Word and your worth in His sight.

Prayer: Dear God, thank You for such a delightful grandchild to think and pray about often! Thank You for also redeeming other hopes and goals in my family. Help us to know what You want us to consider, discuss, and do in the strength of Jesus' name.

Journey with God: Are your thoughts, words, and actions acceptable to God? Journal with Him about needed changes.

Let us think about each other and help each other to show love and do good deeds. You should not stay away from the church meetings, as some are doing. But you should meet together and encourage each other.

Hebrews 10:24–25, NCV

Have you thought about what you'll do to develop outside interests—even if they don't include your family?

Grandparenting marks a big milestone in your life—one that separates you from the early years of parenting. For some, this becomes a trying, even sorrowful, time of change. If devotion to your family's well-being has kept you going for years, you might be afraid you won't be needed anymore.

What would encourage you? For example, if you *like* to be needed, would you be encouraged by a new responsibility in your church? Would you welcome an opportunity to develop a talent that you put on hold while your family was growing up?

To help members of your church and family, you need to be helped too! You'll do good deeds for others after you learn what you can do well. That won't necessarily be what you've always done—deeds arising from necessity or because you have experience. First, you need to experience yourself!

As you consider potential areas of ministry, let God's Word minister to you. Listen to the thoughts He puts on your mind, the situations He brings to your attention, and the old dreams He helps you to recall. Even if you have to go back to school or make other dramatic changes, you can experience the gifts God has given you to develop fully—and fully use!

If you feel shy or fearful about starting something new, you'll need encouragement to keep going. Surround yourself with Christians who will help you have courage to proceed. Meet with them. Pray with them. Worship God with them. Strengthen yourself—and them—by coming together regularly in church.

Prayer: Dear Lord, my family has been so important to me for so long, I've forgotten some things I'd meant to do. Help my plans come together with You so I can be a productive member of the Christian community in Jesus' name.

Journey with God: Take courage from God! Talk with Him about His plans for you to help others and yourself.

But lay up for yourselves treasures in heaven, where neither moth nor rust doth corrupt, and where thieves do not break through nor steal: For where your treasure is, there will your heart be also.

Matthew 6:20–21, KJV

When you're deep in thought your family might ask what's on your mind. If you're worried about bills, eager to earn a better income, or ready to buy an expensive gift for your grandchild, you probably have your mind on money!

As you think about the time, energy, and cash you'll spend to develop a dormant talent or interest, you'll need to ask yourself what's on your heart. Most likely, that won't be money at all!

Money on the heart usually means greed—dollars taken from the mind and pocketed into the center of a person's being. God's children would be out of their minds to do that! But they'd be *thought-less* if they didn't take to heart their family's monetary needs!

Funds placed into your own life insurance or retirement plans protect your child from bearing those expenses later. Once you've tended to basics on your own behalf, you might also consider setting aside monies for your grandchild, perhaps in an annuity or other type of savings program.

If God has gifted you with wealth, rejoice and be glad! Prayerfully consider how to spend, save, and share what you have been given—whether it's money or those talents that you've always meant to take to heart. Since you've devoted your heart to God, you can trust Him to place *His* desires and interests there! Therefore, following your heart may be just what's needed to help you follow and treasure Him.

Prayer: Father, forgive me for not taking seriously the talents and abilities You've put on my heart and in my mind. Help me treasure You and all You've given me in Jesus' name.

Journey with God: Ask God how you can use your talent, time, money, energy, or interests to follow the desires of His heart for you.

___

___

___

___

___

___

___

___

___

___

No one can serve two masters. The person will hate one master and love the other, or will follow one master and refuse to follow the other. You cannot serve both God and worldly riches.

Matthew 6:24, NCV

"I can't do that! My family wouldn't like it. Besides, I'd feel selfish if I did what I really, really wanted."

Here's a bit of irony. In trying to *master* your desires, you become your own master! In submitting to your family's wishes, you *serve*—not God—them.

To serve God, you must trust Him to know which outside interests or talents you're to develop for His use. To follow Him, follow your heart. Even if your mind and body seem distracted, your heart belongs to Him! He's the One who has deposited His interests there on your account! He's the One who has given you talent worth developing, so it would be unappreciative to decline His offer!

If you're not convinced, take another view. As a father, mother, or grandparent, what do you want for your child and, eventually, your grandchild? Do you, for instance, solely value their monetary potential or success? Of course not! Loving your family means you want *more* for them than money.

God also wants more for you. He wants you to use what you've been given. He wants you to develop your interests and abilities so well that they're no longer for your use alone! Instead of only being a pleasant hobby or pastime, your talent can bless other people and help you serve God.

Prayer: Heavenly Father, I don't want to be the servant of my desires, but I also don't want to master what *You've* desired for me! Help me to discern the difference. Help me to seek Your will for me and not be mastered by a habitual need for the approval of my family, friends, or myself! Help me to use *all* that You've given me to serve You in Christ's name.

Journey with God: What's at the center of your life? Your family? Your church? Your desires? If you're not sure, consider how you spend your time, energy, money, and talents. Ask God to help your life and talents center around Him.

___

___

___

___

___

___

___

___

___

A good person gives life to others;
the wise person teaches others
how to live.

Proverbs 11:30, NCV

In these first days of grandparenting, perhaps you've thought a lot about the inheritance you'll leave your family. This can also be an ideal time to think about what you'll bequeath your church.

As you evaluate your financial priorities, you might see a need to set up a living trust or have a new will written. If so, prayerfully consider leaving a portion of your estate to your church home or a ministry whose work you value. This assures you that the monies you earn in your lifetime will continue to benefit others.

Most people don't want to think about dying! They put off simple acts that would take only a few hours of their time but would possibly save their families months, even years, of legal hassles! Or they think they're not worth much financially, so they do nothing, and monies they *could* have left their families becomes part of the state's estate!

Frankly, it's unpleasant to buy insurance and write out a will or instructions for burial! No one wants to think of such things, so you probably don't either. Yet, these acts show you value your family so much, you're willing to undergo a temporary unpleasantry to provide for them for a long time!

The best inheritance you can give your family will be evidence of your belief in God. At times, this may also seem unpleasant, especially if you have to admit your own failures to show how He took care of you! Even though you did nothing to deserve His help, your family will learn that God was still able to work in and through you—despite your flaws!

This teaches that God can do the same for them. This teaches your family how to live in Christ's redeeming love.

Prayer: Heavenly Father, thank You for Your goodness and wisdom that teaches me how to live in Jesus' name.

Journey with God: What unpleasant aspects of life have you avoided? Ask God for His instructions on how you're to face what lies ahead.

Therefore take no thought, saying, What shall we eat? or, What shall we drink? or, Wherewithal shall we be clothed? . . . for your heavenly Father knoweth that ye have need of all these things. But seek ye first the kingdom of God, and his righteousness; and all these things shall be added unto you.

Matthew 6:31–33, KJV

You know what you need: food, clothing, shelter, love. You know what your child and grandchild need too, at least, most of the time! But do you know how *you're needed* by others—not just as a spouse, parent, or grandparent—but as an individual?

As you consider ways to expand your productivity and interests, you'll probably think about other people's needs and how you could be useful. You'll evaluate the ways your time, money, energy, and talent can benefit others, and most of the time, that's great!

By now, however, you might have noticed that God's ways aren't always yours. Just because you feel you *must* or *should* do something doesn't mean it's so as far as God is concerned! Just because the members of your church or family want you to take on a particular task doesn't mean God does.

Everyone on earth needs food, clothing, shelter, and love, but no one person can supply them all! However, needs can be met by the Christian community as each member seeks to hear God before anyone does anything! Instead of rushing ahead so ministries overlap and talents go untapped, seek God first!

Ask Him what He wants you to do. Ask how you're to take part in advancing His kingdom. Seek first the will, way, and Word of God and what He thinks is right for you, and all that you need for His work will be given to you—profusely!

Prayer: Heavenly Father, forgive me for the times I stepped forward to take on a job without first asking You. Help me to see the work *You've* given me to do. Help me to do it well as I feed on Your Word, drink in Your Spirit, and put on Your righteousness in the name and power of Jesus.

Journey with God: What does God want you to do?

Day 82

Children, obey your parents in the Lord, for this is right. "Honor your father and mother"—this is the first commandment with a promise: "so that it may be well with you and you may live long on the earth."

Ephesians 6:1–2, NRSV

"I wish I'd had time to do that when I was younger. Now I just feel too old to develop a talent or new interest."

You're not too old! But, you're not too young either! So, you must be middle-aged, right?

Whether you're thirty-eight or fifty-eight, you're at the age of being caught in the middle! You're trying to find a middle ground somewhere between the wants, needs, and demands of a parent and an adult child. If your mother or father is still alive, you're probably getting advice about what you should do with your time and energy. Chances are good your child has something to say about that too!

These two edges of the generation gap look to you for wisdom, strength, appreciation, and love. Without meaning to, they place expectations on you—often from two different or even opposing views! Since each side has a legitimate viewpoint and rightful claim on your time, it's hard to know what to do or how to fill a gap in both their lives.

Being caught in the middle of two generations can put a squeeze on you! Your child and grandchild need attention, but so does your mom or dad. You want to honor everyone's requests, but sometimes, there isn't enough of you to care for *yourself*—much less embrace anyone else.

As you *honor* a parent you show appreciation and respect. (Your child can do the same for you!) But before you *obey* a person in authority over you, check with your heavenly Parent to be sure it's "in the Lord!" In times of decision making, God can provide counsel from older and younger Christians—godly, ageless people willing to *bring you up* in prayer!

Prayer: Heavenly Father, thank You for the members of my family and church who raise me to You in prayer. Help me to recognize, honor, and obey godly guidance in Jesus' name.

Journey with God: As you consider new areas of interest, talk with God about counsel you've received from other Christians.

Day 83

In that region there were shepherds living in the fields, keeping watch over their flock by night.

Luke 2:8, NRSV

Is God calling you to the mission field in a third world country or the fields around your house and church? Does He want you to devote yourself to the lambs in your family—not just your *grandlamb* or the *kids* who keep straying but those who provide you with ongoing warmth from their love?

In Jesus' day, shepherds probably didn't have impressive possessions or credentials. They didn't aspire to noble tasks or glorious achievements! They were just trying to earn a living! But, as the shepherds took care of their sheep by night, they saw God taking care of His. They saw the good Shepherd, newly come into the world.

Wherever you live and work, God has placed you in a position to keep watch over certain fields. He's given you what's needed to tend your child, grandchild, and others in your family, church home, and Christian community. He's set you over a particular area of responsibility and put you in His charge of a region as you tend, love, and pray for all who meander within your boundaries.

As you expand your territory into a new area of interest or a new use of talent or a new concern outside your family, your task might not seem too ambitious! The Lord may give you solitary chores, such as making a cradle for your grandchild or sewing baby clothes. Yet, as you keep watch over your flock in the region in which you live and work, you too may see the birth of Christ—in the life of your grandchild and others who come into your field.

Prayer: Dear holy Shepherd, thank You for keeping me within the territory of Your love and the boundaries of Your will. Help me to do the same for those You bring into my view in Jesus' name.

Journey with God: What boundaries have you established for yourself? Journey with God around your borders! Talk with Him about the limits you or other people have placed on you and whether those need curtailing or expanding.

Jesus answered,
"Are you looking for me because you saw me do miracles?
No! I tell you the truth.
You are looking for me because you ate the bread and were satisfied."

John 6:26, NCV

"Feed me! Feed me!" Your grandchild can't say those words yet when it's time for a bottle, but people in your church might be saying something similar. Maybe you've heard complaints such as, "I'm not getting fed."

When babies need food, they cry. Grown people who need to be fed might do the same, even though there's usually no need. They could devour God's Word by themselves! They could feed on the Bread of Life through regular communion with the Lord Jesus Christ.

With each new day comes a new need for food. Some days you won't feel much like eating. Other days you'll be famished, and so will the members of your family, church, and community. On different days, people have differing levels of desire. The amount of food that fills a person today might not be the same tomorrow. Yet each can look to Christ—not only to be satisfied but to be filled.

Are you staying filled? Have you devoured the truths Jesus tells—truths He wants your family to understand? Do you hunger for the miracles He has for those who see through eyes of praise? Do you share the bread you've received as you read the Bible each day? Do you tell strangers where God's bread line is or point to the filling power of Jesus Christ?

As you see your level of need and the need of others who wait to be fed, don't look for crumbs and bits of Christ to sustain you! Look for *all* of Him and *all* of His power in the food that lasts forever—the manna made Man.

Prayer: Dear Lord, sometimes I wish I could sit in a high chair and have someone feed me spiritual truths. Help me to help myself to You and bring others to Your table in Christ's name.

Journey with God: Ask God how He wants you to seek Him for Himself—not just in your spare time or at feeding time, but throughout your lifetime!

Day 85

For the Kingdom of God is not a matter of words but of power.

1 Corinthians 4:20, TEV

Since you're a mature member of your family and also of the Christian community, people may turn to you more and more for help. If you're perceived as someone who has all the answers, you might feel overpowered by the needs or demands placed on you. You may see the necessity for setting limits, not on yourself so much as other people.

When your grandchild comes to visit, you create a place of safety by setting limits on his or her mobility. You set cushions around to keep the baby from rolling off the bed or sofa. You make available soft toys that have no easily broken parts or sharp edges.

If you've been getting hurt—falling out of favor with people or crawling wearily to the next task or toddling off without the Lord's permission—you may need to set limits on yourself too! But, if you've said, "No!" to no avail, you may have to reinforce that word with action!

To put power behind your words, you first need to know what word the Lord has given you. Have you asked Him about each new activity, job, or area of responsibility you're to take on or decline? Have you asked Him to set cushions around you to keep you from getting bruised with too much or bored with too little to do? Have you prayed for Him to soften the edges around your moods or interests so you can enjoy harmless and *seemingly* pointless times to relax and play?

Turn each part of your life over to Christ, and you won't get caught up in too many activities or too few. You won't be trapped by promises that could overwhelm you! By waiting for a word from the Word, you'll have a peaceful yet powerful place in the kingdom of God.

Prayer: Heavenly Father, I keep saying I'm going to do this or I'm not going to do that, yet I seem to fall into the same old traps! I guess I'll never have all the answers, but help me remember the questions to ask as I answer Your call to me in Jesus' name.

Journey with God: If Christ is really the answer in your life, what questions are you asking in Him?

____

____

____

____

____

____

____

____

Instead, by speaking the truth in a spirit of love, we must grow up in every way to Christ, who is the head. Under his control all the different parts of the body fit together, and the whole body is held together.

Ephesians 4:15–16, TEV

"Don't ask me to baby-sit! Don't ask me for money! Don't ask me for favors! Don't ask me to bail you out again! Just don't ask me for anything, OK?"

As grandparents begin to seek a life apart from their families, they sometimes overreact! By the time they realize they've had it up to here, they're so emotionally charged, they let their families have it too! That frustration can pack quite a wallop!

To speak the truth in love, you first need to know what the truth is! Unfortunately, very loving Christians may not see resentments or fatigue building. Then, they rail against those they love in an unkind manner that shocks themselves more than anyone else! When a bombardment of offensive words ends, they exclaim, "For goodness sakes! I didn't even know I felt that way!"

If you've been feeling impatient or annoyed with members of your family or church, ask God about the expectations that have been placed on you. Has the help you meant to be for one time only become something that others now expect or demand? Have you been so busy taking care of other people that you've forgotten how to take care of yourself?

Trying to keep your mouth or your temper under control is not the answer! Christ is the answer as you submit the truth about your feelings to Him and place yourself under His control! When you've done that, everything else can't help but come together in a very fitting way!

Prayer: Dear Lord, I thought I wanted to take charge of my life again instead of letting my family and church monopolize my time! Now I see that what I really want is for You to have me completely under Your control in Jesus' name.

Journey with God: Do you feel you're either out of control or manipulated by others? Ask God how you're to get yourself together in Him.

Parents, do not treat your children in such a way as to make them angry. Instead, raise them with Christian discipline and instruction.

Ephesians 6:4, TEV

Once you know God's expectations of you, you'll be able to explain them to members of your family and church. This can free them from dependency on you and enable them to find their own place in the body of Christ.

Although you have already raised your son or daughter, you're now in a better position to help your child raise the level of faith, discernment, or understanding he or she needs for spiritual maturity. This probably won't come by lecturing but by living what you yourself have learned.

To raise your child with Christian instruction, you'll teach what you know to be true. Or, as the old adage goes, you'll "practice what you preach." This won't come from your own bias, but from God's Word as revealed to you.

Raising your child—especially an adult child—with Christian discipline might seem hard, even impossible to do! But this training also involves the practical reality of biblical truth. Punishment and penalties would probably be out of place, but you can continue to establish helpful guidelines in the love, truth, and wisdom of God.

Treating your son or daughter in a wise, realistic, and loving manner will take into account the person he or she is meant to be. This may or may not be what you'd hoped for or expected, but it will be the mature individual God intended. You won't be rearing your child all over again, but you will be raising your son or daughter into Christ.

Prayer: Dear God, help me to raise my child to You in prayer, praise, and thanksgiving! Help me to value and upbring this life in Jesus' name.

Journey with God: Have you treated your grown son or daughter like a child? Have you given more instruction than he or she was mature enough to hear? Ask God to instruct and discipline you in His way to instruct and discipline your child.

God has made us what we are,
and in our union with Christ Jesus
he has created us for a life of good
deeds, which he has already
prepared for us to do.

Ephesians 2:10, TEV

The first few months of grandparenting can seem like a carousel! Like painted ponies on an emotional up-and-down go-round, sometimes you're merry, sometimes not. One day you feel happy and confident about this time and place in your life; the next day, scared, sad, or uncertain.

Around you, the rolling landscape seems familiar, yet also alien and unknown. Right when you think you'll never stand firm and sure again, you're suddenly back to the starting gate, experiencing the joy and excitement you felt the very first time you held your grandchild.

If you have someone with you on this ride—a spouse, another child, a Christian friend, or close proximity to the new family—you're probably enjoying the adventure. If not, you'll find ways to keep in touch with lots of phone calls, letters, tapes, and pictures. But even if you feel alone, you know the Lord stands by the go-round gate, steadying you with His confidence, His strength, His faith in you!

Are you surprised that God believes in you? He does, you know, because He created you. He made you the person you are today. He gave you time, talent, ability, relationships, experiences, and a belief in Him. He knows who you are, and He knows what you're doing!

So, be in Him. Be all you're meant to be. And, whatever you do, do it in Him. You are who you are in the Lord! Thanks be to God!

Prayer: Heavenly Father, Lord and Creator of all, thank You for Your ongoing re-creation of me in Christ Jesus.

Journey with God: Thank God for all He's put into you! List the traits, talents, and beliefs for which you're especially grateful. Thank Him for each part of yourself. Then, listen to Him speak to you about what He's re-creating in you now.

Because the Kingdom of heaven is like this.

Matthew 18:23, TEV

Here's how it is: "Then Peter came to Jesus and asked, 'Lord, if my brother keeps on sinning against me, how many times do I have to forgive him? Seven times?'

"'No, not seven times,' answered Jesus, 'but seventy times seven'" (Matt. 18:21–22, TEV).

Long before a person has forgiven someone four hundred and ninety times, they've probably stopped counting! But, if something really has been forgiven, *it doesn't count anyway!*

Is your life's chalkboard clean? Even if you feel there's too much family history to erase all at once—or even if the chalk dust hasn't yet settled—you've begun these first days of grandparenting in God's kingdom.

Now that your child is a parent, he or she will begin to understand you better. It may take a while! Old issues might surface and old wounds bleed, but, Lord willing, you won't have to deal with them five hundred times! You'll forgive them once—for as many times as it takes.

You'll forgive yourself, too, in God's kingdom. You'll know you don't deserve the goodness He brings. Yet you'll pardon yourself as quickly and as graciously as you can, and you'll go on, eventually arriving at another time when you remember that you're perfectly able to fail.

Your child will fail too, and so will your grandchild as soon as he or she can make choices! That's no excuse, yet each of you will be in good company with every single person in your church, Christian community, and the whole world!

Into the center of the biggest mess, Christ comes. He won't step into all the failures, but He'll walk among all the forgiveness! He will draw you—and those you've forgiven—ever closer and closer, into the kingdom of God.

Prayer: Holy Father, no matter how bad things infuriate or hurt, help me always to forgive in the power of Jesus' name.

Journey with God: If you've had a score to settle or counted on a perfect score from yourself or someone else, it won't add up! Ask God to erase record keeping as you bring members of your family and church to Him in forgiveness and prayer.

____

____

____

____

____

____

Finally, be strong in the Lord and in the strength of his power.

Ephesians 6:10, NRSV

Like most parents, you raised your child the best way you knew at the time. Now, you see that—no matter how much you cared or how skillful you became at parenting, it *couldn't* be good enough!

Everyone has limits beyond which others dare to tread, especially children! Sooner or later, something unexpected comes to tempt or confuse you until you find yourself saying, "Oh, no! I've done it again!"

Yes, you have! But this time is different. This time you're not bringing up a growing child the best way you know how. This time you're upbringing an adult child and a new grandchild in the blessed way that only God knows how!

So, take your devotional time with you. Take your Bible for guidance, comfort, and strength. Take love from God and give it to yourself, your church, and other members of your family. Take His Word with you in prayer.

Prayer: Our Father, Who art in heaven, holy, holy is Your name. Let Your kingdom come. Let Your will be done in my home and church, just as surely as it is in heaven.

Give us this day all that we need to stay spiritually

nourished. And forgive us for being so heavily indebted to others that we forget what we owe You! Help us to forgive as You have forgiven us in Christ Jesus.

Lead us not into the temptation of relying on ourselves or our own experiences, but lead us closer to You. Deliver us from the evil of ever daring or despairing to forget that You—Almighty God—are here.

And, Lord, let this be in Your power, not my strength! Let it be for Your glory, not my need to feel important to my family! Let it be not for my will or wants or needs—not even my desire to be loved. Let it be for the furthering of Your kingdom in my home and the church throughout the world, forever, in Christ's name.

Journey with God: Keep listening to the wonderful plans God has for you and your offspring! Keep praying the prayers He gives you to pray in the name and power of Jesus. Keep journeying with God.